SECOND EDITION

ENGLISH VERBS:
Every Irregular Conjugation

VALERIE HANNAH WEISBERG

Edited by George H. Herrick Ed.D.
Illustrated by Susie Bartz

Copyright 1983 and 1986 Valerie Hannah Weisberg
ISBN 0-9610912-5-8

Library of Congress Catalog Card Number: 85-090269

For information or inquiries, write to:

Valerie Hannah Weisberg
The English Department
Los Angeles Valley College
5800 Fulton Avenue
Van Nuys,
California 91401

Typography by Santa Barbara Graphics
Printed in the U.S.A.

428.2
WE1
1986

Other works by this author include:

Intermediate and Advanced Level Workbooks for *English Verbs: Every Irregular Conjugation*
Language Supplements in *Spanish, French, German, Vietnamese, Japanese* and *Korean.*

Students' Discourse

Three Jolly Stories: ESL, Adult and Child Reader
    The Three Jollys
    Jollys Visit L.A.
    Jolly Gets Mugged

Poems 1984

Capturing Yellow Poems

Introduction

Verbs comprise an extremely important part of the English language, and the mastery of English involves knowing these words and when and how to use them. Unfortunately, many verbs do not follow regular patterns in their various tenses and moods, yet these irregular verbs are frequently used in conversation and writing. Familiarity with these verbs and their varying forms is absolutely essential for anyone striving to achieve true competency in English.

This book not only lists the irregular verbs and conjugates them, but also provides examples of their uses in the various tenses, moods, and voices. Since British and American English differ in some respects, the author has indicated the variations that sometimes occur. This book can thus serve as a helpful guide to students in both the United Kingdom and the United States. The appendix should be of further assistance to those seeking to improve their skills in the language.

English Verbs: Every Irregular Conjugation should prove useful to those from English speaking backgrounds because of its conjugations of the often troublesome irregular verbs. For those for whom English is a second language, the varied material can serve as a reference source and as a complement for formal English instruction. English teachers and librarians will find the book to be a worthwhile addition to their source books on the English language.

George H. Herrick Ed.D. ·
Los Angeles Valley College

i

Preface

This text is the only published collection of every irregular verbs in the English language. The first edition has been bought by libraries, university and college bookstores in most major cities of the United States, England, Canada and Switzerland.

Teachers of English, linguists and librarians are aware of an overwhelming need to improve the fundamental skills of English. The book was compiled to answer this need and to provide the first complete dictionary of every irregular verb conjugation.

This new edition has been extended to facilitate self-study and aid students facing examinations on fundamental skills of English, like G.C.E in England SAT and TOEFL in the United States.

The first two columns show each verb conjugation; the third provides a marginal cross-referenced index and, when relevant, parenthetical comments on the verbs. As in the first edition, to avoid confusion with the simple past, the past participles and British variants are noted on the top left side of the page.

Besides examples of regular, "Y" ending and passive voice conjugations, the appendix now includes a list of the copulative or linking verbs, verb scramblers and other exercises, devised for self-testing, with an answer key.

Language translations in Spanish, Thai, Korean, Japanese, Vietnamese, German and French are available in inexpensive supplements. This book, therefore, serves as an especially useful guide to students of English as a second language as well as providing an easy reference text for writers, teachers, librarians and all students of American and British English.

Valerie Hannah Weisberg MA
Los Angeles Valley College

ACKNOWLEDGEMENTS

I am especially grateful for the help and encouragement of Natalie Beaumont, Prapai Bonruang, Michael Collyer, Lee L. Davis, James Isaacs, Roselle M. Lewis, Theodore Martin, Edythe McGovern, Susanne Medina, Patricia Nichols, Martha Pennington, William Richardson, Susan Shields, Stephen Statham, Joseph Stewart, Kenneth Warfield, David, Jonathan and Seymour Weisberg, Rita Werner and all of my friends, students and colleagues at Los Angeles Valley College, the University of California, Santa Barbara and Santa Barbara Public Library.

To the Teacher

Naturally, the idea of presenting our verbal system to a non-English speaking student who may never before have been exposed to a more formal education, is a formidable task, and certainly this text, *English Verbs: Every Irregular Conjugation,* can only be used once the basic skills of reading and comprehension have been attained. However, for the intermediate, advanced and native speaking students who are familiar with our regular verb system, there are many activities which will expose them to the irregulars and which will expand and enrich their vocabulary, writing and communication skills.

Most teachers of English, linguists and specialists of English as a second language agree that verbs are the matrix of a language. Hence, the necessity of establishing this basic foundation cannot be ignored. To simplify and to create an atmosphere of enjoyment during the learning process is the vital task of the individual teacher. However, activities which have proved successful when used with this text include: oral quizzing, drilling, chanting, role-playing, writing other "Y" ending and regular verbs— not listed in the appendix—and completing the fill-ins given in the workbook exercises.

Teachers who are able to work with smaller groups have found "verb rummy" a popular and enjoyable activity. Once students have collected three or more verb families and written them on index cards, they can simulate the game of rummy. The levels of difficulties are established by the verb family sets used and the number of cards dealt. A beginning group might work with four cards and collect pairs; an advanced group might play with eleven cards and collect sets of three to a complete family of eleven. Another pursuit is to find out how many of the past participles act as adjectives. For example, "The *torn* shirt," but not "The *ran* boy." The main purpose is to encourage students to use the text, thereby giving them exposure to the more commonly misused verbs in the English language. The fill-in exercises are also another means of having students seek and find for practice and reinforcement.

For non-English speakers, unfamiliar with our verb tense system, it might be worthwhile to compare our tense with another system in terms of REAL and UNREAL. The present tense in this system represents the actual ongoing reality of events that are existing and can be readily and immediately ascertained. The modals, perfect or progressive conjugations are not under this system, but are reserved for the UNREAL situations of the subjunctive and conditional moods.

REAL   Present and past tenses in all forms.

UNREAL   Future, conditional and subjunctive forms (all pertain to unreal situations which have not yet occurred) or the imperative form which suggest an expectation that has not yet been ascertained or fulfilled.

The main purpose of this text is to establish a meaningful pattern for the families of verb tenses and to serve as an invaluable resource for students to find answers easily with a minimum of frustration. We all realize that learning another language is difficult enough without compounding the problem by making our verb system illogical and elusive. By sorting out every irregular verb, the student will become more aware of how amazingly regular many of them really are!

*To my mother, sons
and in loving memory of my father.*

CONTENTS

VERBS

These words form the essential part of a sentence or clause, and are considered by linguists as the matrix of language. Verbs often show action and can stand alone as a sentence or complete the meaning or denote the action of its subject in a sentence. Grammarians refer to these as the predicate or verb phrase of a sentence, and this term encompasses all forms of the verb as well as its object, adverbial phrase or subject complement. (See Copulative or Linking Verbs in the appendix.)

MOODS

Moods are groups of verb forms which show how the action is viewed by the speaker or writer. They are the INDICATIVE, the CONDITIONAL, the SUBJUNCTIVE and the IMPERATIVE.

INDICATIVE
The indicative mood is used in declarative or in interrogative sentences. For example, "The sun shines," or "Is the wind blowing?"

CONDITIONAL
The conditional mood expresses the condition of possibility for the future. *Could, would and should* are placed in front of the verb and tentatively answer questions posed by "if" and "when." Statements like, "I could find it if I had a good map," suggest conditional ability, or "I should go tomorrow" suggest that the speaker is obliged to go but may find a reason for not going. In general, *would* is used most often in situations involving volition (the intention, wish or desire to do something) and *should* and *ought* are reserved for situations of obligation.

SUBJUNCTIVE
The subjunctive mood is used for indirect commands or to indicate supposition, condition, purpose, possibility, uncertainty, contingency, desire, exultation and expectation usually introduced by *if, may* or *might, except, that, unless, lest* or *until*. For the present tense use the stem (infinitive without *to*) of the verb for all persons except the verb *to be* which uses *were* for all persons in the present tense. For example, "If I *were* twice as strong, I still couldn't lift that box." For past tense, use *might* before the stem, "He *might* be strong."

IMPERATIVE
The imperative mood is used for a command or request with the stem only. The second person "you" is implied often forming a one word sentence. For example, "Sit," or "Bring the book," or "Be quiet." Often the personal pronoun may be added for emphasis. For example, "You bring the book." This form is not considered polite for general usage. The conditional *would* is usually placed in front of the verb to form a request. "*Would* you bring the book?"

VOICE

Voice shows whether the subject acts (active) or is acted upon (passive):

ACTIVE VOICE
The subject is doing the action of the verb. For example, "They baked cakes." They (*subject*) baked (*verb*) cakes (*object of the verb*).

PASSIVE VOICE
This form shows the subject as receiving the action of the verb. For example, "Cakes are baked."

Note that this form takes the auxiliary of the verb *to be* and sometimes the auxiliary of *to get* and joins it with the past participle of the main verb, in this case bake. Here, the auxiliary forms the tense and is conjugated. The main verb is always shown in its past participle form.

EMPHATIC VOICE

In the indicative or interrrogative mood, the verb form of *to do* precedes the main verb to add emphasis to a statement. For example, "He *does* eat," or *do* precedes the subject to form the question, "Does *he eat?*" As with all auxiliaries *do* is conjugated, and the main verb then follows in its stem form. Note that like *have* and *be, do* also functions as a main verb to form sentences which repeat the word. Such as, "They do (*auxiliary*) do (*main verb:* prepare, work, make or bring to pass) it." Notice that the auxiliary changes depending on the tense or person, for example, "Jonathan *does* do extra work" or "Yesterday, David *did* eat breakfast." Unlike all other auxiliaries *do* forms a complete sentence without the subject when combined with the imperative to form the emphatic command, "Do eat." When the subject precedes the verb stem, the sentence is always interrogative. For example, "Do the *British* always *have* tea in the afternoon?"

AUXILIARIES

MODALS		TENSE[1]	VOICE
Must	Ought	Have	Be[2]
Might	Should	Shall	Do
May	Would	Will	Get[3]
Can	Could		

Modals followed by the stem (except for *ought*, which retains *to*) form a verb phrase. These phrases are used to express possibility, liberty, permission, obligation or necessity. They are known also as "helping verbs" because they help the stem form its meaning. Those known as modals do not inflect (change) except for *shall, will,* and *have* which do so in order to show tense.

Can or *could* indicate ability. "I can work that computer."

May or *might* are used for permission. *May* is used to indicate a wish. "May we have peace?", "May I have a chocolate sundae?" or "Might I have done that?

Must expresses obligation or necessity. "I must work to feed my family."

Shall is always used in first person questions. "Shall I make coffee?" In very formal speech it is used to express futurity in the first person and volition or determination, obligation or necessity in the second or third persons. "I shall accept the appointment," or "You shall go to school."

---

[1] *Shall, will* and *have* also function as modals when used to express volition. "You *have* to eat." (Have is also a main verb.)
[2] *Be* functions in three ways. It is a main verb and an auxiliary verb forming the progressive tense and the passive voice.
[3] *Get* in colloquial usage is an auxiliary forming the progressive tense. For example, "Let's *get* going," and for the passive voice (present or past tense), "Let's *get* done," or "It *got* done."

Will[4] in very formal speech expresses determination or obligation in the first person and futurity in the second and third persons. "I will win that race."

Have, has, or *had* precede the stem to form the perfect tense.

Would may express habitual past action or willingness. "I would write everyday," or "I would help him if he needed it."

Ought and *should* express duty or obligation or expectation. "That work ought to be finished by tonight," "Children should eat less junk food."

Be, is, are, was, or *were* precede the stem to form the progressive tense and the passive voice. "I am going home," or "War was avoided."

Do, does, or *did* precede the stem to form the emphatic voice. For example, "I do eat chocolate even though it makes me fat." Also known as the "dumb do" or "colourless auxiliary"[5] when preceding *not* to form a negative statement. "He *does* not plan to be a doctor," or when it precedes the subject to form a question, "*Does* he plan to be a doctor?" *Be, have* and all the modals also precede *not* to form negative statements:

She *hasn't* (has not) eaten chocolate.

She *must, would, can* or *will* not or *ought* not to eat chocolate.

Or they precede the subject to form questions:

Ought she to eat chocolate?

Is he strong enough?

Have we strength enough?

Can or *will* we work hard enough?

Must we go?

Should, would or *could* we fight for our rights?

VERB TENSES

For non-English speakers, unfamiliar with our verb tense system, we might compare our tenses with other systems in terms of REAL and UNREAL time. The present tense in this system represents the

---

[4]In American English *will* is now generally accepted for all persons in the future tense, "I *will* leave." or "They *will* arrive."
[5]Fowler, H.W. *Dictionary of Modern English Usage.* 2nd Ed. Rev. Sir Ernest Gowers, 1965 (p.136).

actual ongoing reality of events that are existing and can be readily and immediately ascertained. The modals, perfect or progressive conjugations are reserved for the UNREAL situations of the subjunctive and conditional moods.

    REAL   Present and past tenses in all forms

    UNREAL   Future, conditional, subjunctive (all pertain to unreal situations which have not yet occurred) or imperative forms suggest an expectation that has not yet been fulfilled.

In English, the time in which an action or state occurs is indicated by the verb tense. The three main aspects of time are reflected by PRESENT TENSE, PAST TENSE and FUTURE TENSE. The present tense is normally formed by taking the stem[6] of the infinitive and adding *s* or *es* for the third person singular. The past tense of regular verbs is formed by adding *ed* or *d* to the stem of the verb. The irregular verbs[7], however, do not follow this pattern and should be memorized. The future requires *shall* or *will* to precede the stem. The other tenses are the PROGRESSIVE and the PERFECT. We add *ing* to the stem to form the progressive or present participle and *ed*, or *t* to form the simple past or the past participle for the perfect tense or passive voice constructions. Note that the auxiliaries of "have" and "be" are conjugated as helpers to the main verb. The following illustrates actions which require different verb tenses.

---

[6]The infinitive is always expressed by *to* and the stem of the verb. For example, *to eat*.

[7]Many irregular past participles, however, end in *n*. I *have known* him for years," or "He *was known* for years."

PRESENT TENSE
This is used to show an action that is now taking place; or a state or circumstance which is now existing; or a general situation which is habitual or recurring.

"I eat."

PRESENT PROGRESSIVE OR CONTINUOUS TENSE
This is also used to express an action in the present that is progressive or continuous and that has not yet been completed.

"I'm eating."

PAST TENSE
This indicates a completed action or a state of being gone by or just past.

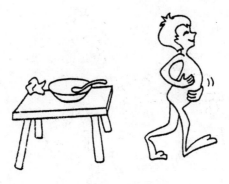

"I ate."

PAST PROGRESSIVE TENSE
This indicates a continuing action or state of being that is now completed, or an action that was in progress at a former time now past or just gone by.

"I was eating."

FUTURE TENSE
This is indicated by anticipating an action or circumstance or state to come.

"I will eat."

PRESENT PERFECT OR PRESENT PERFECT PROGRESSIVE TENSE:
This indicates an action that has been completed or has been in progress in the past.

"I have eaten." or "I have been eating.

PAST PERFECT OR PROGRESSIVE TENSE:

This indicates an action that has been completed or had been in progress in the past before another action.

"I had eaten, but I was still hungry," or
"I had been eating, but I still needed more."

FUTURE PERFECT OR PROGRESSIVE TENSE

This expresses an action or state that will be completed or that will be continuing in the future before another anticipated action of the future.

"I will have finished breakfast before I get to the office," or
"By eight, I will have been eating and drinking for an hour," or
"I will have eaten 365 breakfasts by next year."

IMPERATIVE, COMMAND OR EMPHATIC COMMAND

This reflects an immediate present tense. It is always indicated by the stem of the infinitive verb. *Do* precedes the stem to give extra emphasis to the command. Hence, the imperative with *do* is often referred to as the *emphatic command*. The second person, *you* is implied or understood; however, when it is included with the stem alone, it adds emphasis. The politer form always includes *would* and often *please*. "Would you eat," or "Please eat."

"Eat, or Do eat."

PRESENT OR PAST PASSIVE VOICE CONSTRUCTION

This displaces the subject and shows the object as receiving the action.

Breakfast is or was eaten.

ABIDE

Past Participles: abided, abode (literary)

Indicative Present Tense

I abide	We abide
You abide	You abide
One[2] abides	They abide

Past Tense

I abode	We abode
You abode	You abode
One abode	They abode

Future Tense

I[3] shall abide	We shall abide
You will abide	You will abide
One will abide	They will abide

Present or Past Progressive Tense

I[4] am or was abiding	We are or were abiding
You are or were abiding	You are or were abiding
One is or was abiding	They are or were abiding

Future Progressive Tense

I shall be abiding	We shall be abiding
You will be abiding	You will be abiding
One will be abiding	They will be abiding

Present or Past Perfect Tense

I[5] have or had abided	We have or had abided
You have or had abided	You have or had abided
One has or had abided	They have or had abided

Future Perfect Tense

I[3] shall have abided	We shall have abided
You will have abided	You will have abided
One will have abided	They will have abided

Future Perfect Progressive Tense

I shall have been abiding	We shall have been abiding
You will have been abiding	You will have been abiding
One will have been abiding	They will have been abiding

ABIDE[1]
(also regular)

ARISE
(see RISE)

ALIGHT
(see LIGHT)

---

[1] Same conjugations for BIDE.
[2] Also she, he, it.
[3] Often contracted: I'll, you'll, he'll, she'll, we'll, or they'll (shall not: shan't, will not: won't).
[4] Often contracted: I'm, you're, we're, or they're.
[5] Often contracted: I've or I'd, you've or you'd, we've or we'd, or they've or they'd.

Present or Past Perfect Progressive Tense

I have or had been abiding
You have or had been abiding
One has or had been abiding

We have or had been abiding
You have or had been abiding
They have or had been abiding

Conditional (would, should or could)

I[1] would abide
You would abide
One would abide

We would abide
You would abide
They would abide

Conditional Progressive Tense

I would be abiding
You would be abiding
One would be abiding

We would be abiding
You would be abiding
They would be abiding

Conditional Perfect Tense

I would have abided
You would have abided
One would have abided

We would have abided
You would have abided
They would have abided

Conditional Perfect Progressive Tense

I would have been abiding
You would have been abiding
One would have been abiding

We would have been abiding
You would have been abiding
They would have been abiding

Subjunctive Present or Past Tense

I may or might abide
You may or might abide
One may or might abide

We may or might abide
You may or might abide
They may or might abide

Subjunctive Present or Past Perfect Tense

I may[2] or might have abided
You may or might have abided
One may or might have abided

We may or might have abided
You may or might have abided
They may or might have abided

Subjunctive Present or Past Perfect Progressive Tense

I may or might have been abiding
You may or might have been abiding
One may or might have been abiding

We may or might have been abiding
You may or might have been abiding
They may or might have been abiding

Imperative
(You) abide (it.)

---

[1] Often contracted: I'd, you'd, we'd, he'd, she'd, they'd.
[2] Subjunctive mood, p.1

AWAKE

Past Participles: awoken, awaked and awoke (rare, British)

Indicative Present Tense

I awake	We awake
You awake	You awake
One[2] awakes	They awake

Past Tense

I awoke	We awoke
You awoke	You awoke
One awoke	They awoke

Future Tense

I[3] shall awake	We shall awake
You will awake	You will awake
One will awake	They will awake

Present or Past Progressive Tense

I[4] am or was awaking	We are or were awaking
You are or were awaking	You are or were awaking
One is or was awaking	They are or were awaking

Future Progressive Tense

I shall be awaking	We shall be awaking
You will be awaking	You will be awaking
One will be awaking	They will be awaking

Present or Past Perfect Tense

I[5] have or had awoken	We have or had awoken
You have or had awoken	You have or had awoken
One has or had awoken	They have or had awoken

Future Perfect Tense

I[3] shall have awoken	We shall have awoken
You will have awoken	You will have awoken
One will have awoken	They will have awoken

Future Perfect Progressive Tense

I shall have been awaking	We shall have been awaking
You will have been awaking	You will have been awaking
One will have been awaking	They will have been awaking

AWAKE[1]
(also regular)

AWAKEN
(separate,
regular verb.)

BACKBITE
(see BITE)

BACKSLIDE
(see SLIDE)

---

[1] Same conjugations for WAKE.
[2] Also she, he, it.
[3] Often contracted: I'll, you'll, he'll, she'll, we'll, or they'll (shall not: shan't; will not: won't).
[4] Often contracted: I'm, you're, we're, or they're.
[5] Often contracted: I've or I'd, you've or you'd, we've or we'd, or they've or they'd.

Present or Past Perfect Progressive Tense

I have or had been awaking	We have or had been awaking
You have or had been awaking	You have or had been awaking
One has or had been awaking	They have or had been awaking

Conditional (would, should or could)

I[1] would awake	We would awake
You would awake	You would awake
One would awake	They would awake

Conditional Progressive Tense

I would be awaking	We would be awaking
You would be awaking	You would be awaking
One would be awaking	They would be awaking

Conditional Perfect Tense

I would have awoken	We would have awoken
You would have awoken	You would have awoken
One would have awoken	They would have awoken

Conditional Perfect Progressive Tense

I would have been awaking	We would have been awaking
You would have been awaking	You would have been awaking
One would have been awaking	They would have been awaking

Subjunctive Present or Past Tense

I may or might awake	We may or might awake
You may or might awake	You may or might awake
One may or might awake	They may or might awake

Subjunctive Present or Past Perfect Tense

I may[2] or might have awoken	We may or might have awoken
You may or might have awoken	You may or might have awoken
One may or might have awoken	They may or might have awoken

Subjunctive Present or Past Perfect Progressive Tense

I may or might have been awaking	We may or might have been awaking
You may or might have been awaking	You may or might have been awaking
One may or might have been awaking	They may or might have been awaking

Imperative
(You) awake (it), or (you) wake up.

---

[1] Often contracted: I'd, you'd, we'd, he'd, she'd, they'd.
[2] Subjunctive mood, p.1

Past Participle: been

Indicative Present Tense

I am	We are
You are	You are
One[1] is	They are

Past Tense

I was	We were
You were	You were
One was	They were

Future Tense

I[2] shall be	We shall be
You will be	You will be
One will be	They will be

Present or Past Progressive Tense

I[3] am or was being	We are or were being
You are or were being	You are or were being
One is or was being	They are or were being

Future Progressive Tense

I shall be being	We shall be being
You will be being	You will be being
One will be being	They will be being

Present or Past Perfect Tense

I[4] have or had been	We have or had been
You have or had been	You have or had been
One has or had been	They have or had been

Future Perfect Tense

I[2] shall have been	We shall have been
You will have been	You will have been
One will have been	They will have been

Future Perfect Progressive Tense

I shall have been being	We shall have been being
You will have been being	You will have been being
One will have been being	They will have been being

BE

Like *do* and *have,* *be* functions as an auxiliary (p.2) as well as a main verb meaning to possess a sense or state of existence, "To be or not to be . . ." (Hamlet's famous soliloquy), or as a copulative or linking verb.

In the progressive form this verb is often semantically constrained and forms rarely used conjugations. Possibly the awkward sounding alliteration of "be being" and "been being" has caused this avoidance.

The Emphatic Command (p.8) also takes this constraint; *be* is never combined alone with *do.* For example, "Do be kind to them," but never, "Do be."

Formal tradition requires a subject pronoun after any form of *be.* For example, "It is *he, she* or *I.*"

---

[1] Also she, he, it.
[2] Often contracted: I'll, you'll, he'll, she'll, we'll, or they'll (shall not: shan't, will not: won't).
[3] Often contracted: I'm, you're, we're, or they're.
[4] Often contracted: I've or I'd, you've or you'd, we've or we'd, or they've or they'd.

15

Present or Past Perfect Progressive Tense

I have or had been being

You have or had been being

One has or had been being

We have or had been being

You have or had been being

They have or had been being

Conditional (would, should or could)

I[1] would be

You would be

One would be

We would be

You would be

They would be

Conditional Progressive Tense

I would be being

You would be being

One would be being

We would be being

You would be being

They would be being

Conditional Perfect Tense

I would have been

You would have been

One would have been

We would have been

You would have been

They would have been

Conditional Perfect Progressive Tense

I would have been being

You would have been being

One would have been being

We would have been being

You would have been being

They would have been being

Subjunctive Present or Past Tense

I may or might be

You may or might be

One may or might be

We may or might be

You may or might be

They may or might be

Subjunctive Present or Past Perfect Tense

I may[2] or might have been

You may or might have been

One may or might have been

We may or might have been

You may or might have been

They may or might have been

Subjunctive Present or Past Perfect Progressive Tense

I may or might have been being

You may or might have been being

One may or might have been being

We may or might have been being

You may or might have been being

They may or might have been being

Imperative

(You) be (it: informal usage only).

---

[1] Often contracted: I'd, you'd, we'd, he'd, she'd, they'd.

[2] Subjunctive mood, p.1

Past Participles: born (to give or receive birth), borne (to carry a burden)

Indicative Present Tense

I bear	We bear	
You bear	You bear	
One[2] bears	They bear	

Past Tense

I bore	We bore
You bore	You bore
One bore	They bore

Future Tense

I[3] shall bear	We shall bear
You will bear	You will bear
One will bear	They will bear

Present or Past Progressive Tense

I[4] am or was bearing	We are or were bearing
You are or were bearing	You are or were bearing
One is or was bearing	They are or were bearing

Future Progressive Tense

I shall be bearing	We shall be bearing
You will be bearing	You will be bearing
One will be bearing	They will be bearing

Present or Past Perfect Tense

I[5] have or had born	We have or had born
You have or had born	You have or had born
One has or had born	They have or had born

Future Perfect Tense

I[3] shall have born	We shall have born
You will have born	You will have born
One will have born	They will have born

Future Perfect Progressive Tense

I shall have been bearing	We shall have been bearing
You will have been bearing	You will have been bearing
One will have been bearing	They will have been bearing

BEAR[1]

BEAT
(also invariable,
see appendix)

BECOME
(see COME)

BEFALL
(see FALL)

BEGET
(see GET)

---

[1] Same conjugations for FORESWEAR, SHEAR (also regular, past *shore,* dialectical),
SWEAR, TEAR *(p.p. torn)*, WEAR *(p.p. worn)*.
[2] Also she, he, it.
[3] Often contracted: I'll, you'll, he'll, she'll, we'll, or they'll (shall not: shan't, will not: won't).
[4] Often contracted: I'm, you're, we're, or they're.
[5] Often contracted: I've or I'd, you've or you'd, we've or we'd, or they've or they'd.

Present or Past Perfect Progressive Tense

I have or had been bearing	We have or had been bearing
You have or had been bearing	You have or had been bearing
One has or had been bearing	They have or had been bearing

Conditional (would, should or could)

I[1] would bear	We would bear
You would bear	You would bear
One would bear	They would bear

Conditional Progressive Tense

I would be bearing	We would be bearing
You would be bearing	You would be bearing
One would be bearing	They would be bearing

Conditional Perfect Tense

I would have born	We would have born
You would have born	You would have born
One would have born	They would have born

Conditional Perfect Progressive Tense

I would have been bearing	We would have been bearing
You would have been bearing	You would have been bearing
One would have been bearing	They would have been bearing

Subjunctive Present or Past Tense

I may or might bear	We may or might bear
You may or might bear	You may or might bear
One may or might bear	They may or might bear

Subjunctive Present or Past Perfect Tense

I may[2] or might have born	We may or might have born
You may or might have born	You may or might have born
One may or might have born	They may or might have born

Subjunctive Present or Past Perfect Progressive Tense

I may or might have been bearing	We may or might have been bearing
You may or might have been bearing	You may or might have been bearing
One may or might have been bearing	They may or might have been bearing

Imperative
(You) bear it.

---

[1] Often contracted: I'd, you'd, we'd, he'd, she'd, they'd.
[2] Subjunctive mood, p.1

BEGIN

Past Participle: begun

Indicative Present Tense

I begin	We begin
You begin	You begin
One[2] begins	They begin

Past Tense

I began	We began
You began	You began
One began	They began

Future Tense

I[3] shall begin	We shall begin
You will begin	You will begin
One will begin	They will begin

Present or Past Progressive Tense

I[4] am or was beginning	We are or were beginning
You are or were beginning	You are or were beginning
One is or was beginning	They are or were beginning

Future Progressive Tense

I shall be beginning	We shall be beginning
You will be beginning	You will be beginning
One will be beginning	They will be beginning

Present or Past Perfect Tense

I[5] have or had begun	We have or had begun
You have or had begun	You have or had begun
One has or had begun	They have or had begun

Future Perfect Tense

I[3] shall have begun	We shall have begun
You will have begun	You will have begun
One will have begun	They will have begun

Future Perfect Progressive Tense

I shall have been beginning	We shall have been beginning
You will have been beginning	You will have been beginning
One will have been beginning	They will have been beginning

BEGIN

BEHOLD
(See HOLD)

BELAY
(regular,
see appendix)

---

[1] Same conjugations for DRINK, RING, SHRINK, SING, SINK, SPIN (rare, only British: *past* span), SPRING STINK, SWIM.
[2] Also she, he, it.
[3] Often contracted: I'll, you'll, he'll, she'll, we'll, or they'll (shall not: shan't, will not: won't).
[4] Often contracted: I'm, you're, we're, or they're.
[5] Often contracted: I've or I'd, you've or you'd, we've or we'd, or they've or they'd.

Present or Past Perfect Progressive Tense

I have or had been beginning
You have or had been beginning
One has or had been beginning   .

We have or had been beginning
You have or had been beginning
They have or had been beginning

Conditional (would, should or could)

I[1] would begin
You would begin
One would begin

We would begin
You would begin
They would begin

Conditional Progressive Tense

I would be beginning
You would be beginning
One would be beginning

We would be beginning
You would be beginning
They would be beginning

Conditional Perfect Tense

I would have begun
You would have begun
One would have begun

We would have begun
You would have begun
They would have begun

Conditional Perfect Progressive Tense

I would have been beginning
You would have been beginning
One would have been beginning

We would have been beginning
You would have been beginning
They would have been beginning

Subjunctive Present or Past Tense

I may or might begin
You may or might begin
One may or might begin

We may or might begin
You may or might begin
They may or might begin

Subjunctive Present or Past Perfect Tense

I may[2] or might have begun
You may or might have begun
One may or might have begun

We may or might have begun
You may or might have begun
They may or might have begun

Subjunctive Present or Past Perfect Progressive Tense

I may or might have been beginning
You may or might have been beginning
One may or might have been beginning

We may or might have been beginning
You may or might have been beginning
They may or might have been beginning

Imperative
(You) begin (it.)

---

[1] Often contracted: I'd, you'd, we'd, he'd, she'd, they'd.
[2] Subjunctive mood, p.1

BEND

Past Participle: bent

Indicative Present Tense

I bend	We bend
You bend	You bend
One[2] bends	They bend

Past Tense

I bent	We bent
You bent	You bent
One bent	They bent

Future Tense

I[3] shall bend	We shall bend
You will bend	You will bend
One will bend	They will bend

Present or Past Progressive Tense

I[4] am or was bending	We are or were bending
You are or were bending	You are or were bending
One is or was bending	They are or were bending

Future Progressive Tense

I shall be bending	We shall be bending
You will be bending	You will be bending
One will be bending	They will be bending

Present or Past Perfect Tense

I[5] have or had bent	We have or had bent
You have or had bent	You have or had bent
One has or had bent	They have or had bent

Future Perfect Tense

I[3] shall have bent	We shall have bent
You will have bent	You will have bent
One will have bent	They will have bent

Future Perfect Progressive Tense

I shall have been bending	We shall have been bending
You will have been bending	You will have been bending
One will have been bending	They will have been bending

BEND[1]
(regular,
see appendix)

BEREAVE
(also regular
see LEAVE)

BESEECH
(also regular
see BRING)

BESPEAK
(see SPEAK)

BESTEAD
(literary, regular
and invariable
p.p. bested)

BESTREW
(see MOW)

BESTRIDE
(see RIDE)

BET
(invariable
see appendix)

BETAKE
(see TAKE)

---

[1] Same conjugations for LEND, REND, SEND, SHEND, SPEND, WEND (archaic, old past tense, *went*, now merged with *go*. Also a regular verb.)
[2] Also she, he, it.
[3] Often contracted: I'll, you'll, he'll, she'll, we'll, or they'll (shall not: shan't, will not: won't).
[4] Often contracted: I'm, you're, we're, or they're.
[5] Often contracted: I've or I'd, you've or you'd, we've or we'd, or they've or they'd.

Present or Past Perfect Progressive Tense

I have or had been bending
You have or had been bending
One has or had been bending

We have or had been bending
You have or had been bending
They have or had been bending

Conditional (would, should or could)

I[1] would bend
You would bend
One would bend

We would bend
You would bend
They would bend

Conditional Progressive Tense

I would be bending
You would be bending
One would be bending

We would be bending
You would be bending
They would be bending

Conditional Perfect Tense

I would have bent
You would have bent
One would have bent

We would have bent
You would have bent
They would have bent

Conditional Perfect Progressive Tense

I would have been bending
You would have been bending
One would have been bending

We would have been bending
You would have been bending
They would have been bending

Subjunctive Present or Past Tense

I may or might bend
You may or might bend
One may or might bend

We may or might bend
You may or might bend
They may or might bend

Subjunctive Present or Past Perfect Tense

I may[2] or might have bent
You may or might have bent
One may or might have bent

We may or might have bent
You may or might have bent
They may or might have bent

Subjunctive Present or Past Perfect Progressive Tense

I may or might have been bending
You may or might have been bending
One may or might have been bending

We may or might have been bending
You may or might have been bending
They may or might have been bending

Imperative
(You) bend (it).

---

[1] Often contracted: I'd, you'd, we'd, he'd, she'd, they'd.
[2] Subjunctive mood, p.1

BID

Past Participles: bidden, bid (auction), bade (American)

BID[1]
(Also invariable)

BIDE
(see ABIDE)

Indicative Present Tense

I bid	We bid
You bid	You bid
One[2] bids	They bid

Past Tense (bid, bad [British])

I bade	We bade
You bade	You bade
One bade	They bade

Future Tense

I[3] shall bid	We shall bid
You will bid	You will bid
One will bid	They will bid

Present or Past Progressive Tense

I[4] am or was bidding	We are or were bidding
You are or were bidding	You are or were bidding
One is or was bidding	They are or were bidding

Future Progressive Tense

I shall be bidding	We shall be bidding
You will be bidding	You will be bidding
One will be bidding	They will be bidding

Present or Past Perfect Tense

I[5] have or had bidden	We have or had bidden
You have or had bidden	You have or had bidden
One has or had bidden	They have or had bidden

Future Perfect Tense

I[3] shall have bidden	We shall have bidden
You will have bidden	You will have bidden
One will have bidden	They will have bidden

Future Perfect Progressive Tense

I shall have been bidding	We shall have been bidding
You will have been bidding	You will have been bidding
One will have been bidding	They will have been bidding

---

[1] Same conjugations for FORBID.
[2] Also she, he, it.
[3] Often contracted: I'll, you'll, he'll, she'll, we'll, or they'll (shall not: shan't, will not: won't).
[4] Often contracted: I'm, you're, we're, or they're.
[5] Often contracted: I've or I'd, you've or you'd, we've or we'd, or they've or they'd.

Present or Past Perfect Progressive Tense

I have or had been bidding	We have or had been bidding
You have or had been bidding	You have or had been bidding
One has or had been bidding	They have or had been bidding

Conditional (would, should or could)

I[1] would bid	We would bid
You would bid	You would bid
One would bid	They would bid

Conditional Progressive Tense

I would be bidding	We would be bidding
You would be bidding	You would be bidding
One would be bidding	They would be bidding

Conditional Perfect Tense

I would have bidden	We would have bidden
You would have bidden	You would have bidden
One would have bidden	They would have bidden

Conditional Perfect Progressive Tense

I would have been bidding	We would have been bidding
You would have been bidding	You would have been bidding
One would have been bidding	They would have been bidding

Subjunctive Present or Past Tense

I may or might bid	We may or might bid
You may or might bid	You may or might bid
One may or might bid	They may or might bid

Subjunctive Present or Past Perfect Tense

I may[2] or might have bidden	We may or might have bidden
You may or might have bidden	You may or might have bidden
One may or might have bidden	They may or might have bidden

Subjunctive Present or Past Perfect Progressive Tense

I may or might have been bidding	We may or might have been bidding
You may or might have been bidding	You may or might have been bidding
One may or might have been bidding	They may or might have been bidding

Imperative
(You) bid (it).

---

[1] Often contracted: I'd, you'd, we'd, he'd, she'd, they'd.
[2] Subjunctive mood, p.1

Past Participle: bound

Indicative Present Tense

I bind	We bind
You bind	You bind
One[2] binds	They bind

Past Tense

I bound	We bound
You bound	You bound
One bound	They bound

Future Tense

I[3] shall bind	We shall bind
You will bind	You will bind
One will bind	They will bind

Present or Past Progressive Tense

I[4] am or was binding	We are or were binding
You are or were binding	You are or were binding
One is or was binding	They are or were binding

Future Progressive Tense

I shall be binding	We shall be binding
You will be binding	You will be binding
One will be binding	They will be binding

Present or Past Perfect Tense

I[5] have or had bound	We have or had bound
You have or had bound	You have or had bound
One has or had bound	They have or had bound

Future Perfect Tense

I[3] shall have bound	We shall have bound
You will have bound	You will have bound
One will have bound	They will have bound

Future Perfect Progressive Tense

I shall have been binding	We shall have been binding
You will have been binding	You will have been binding
One will have been binding	They will have been binding

---

[1] Same conjugations for SPELLBIND, FIND, GRIND, WIND.
[2] Also she, he, it.
[3] Often contracted: I'll, you'll, he'll, she'll, we'll, or they'll (shall not: shan't, will not: won't).
[4] Often contracted: I'm, you're, we're, or they're.
[5] Often contracted: I've or I'd, you've or you'd, we've or we'd, or they've or they'd.

Present or Past Perfect Progressive Tense

I have or had been binding
You have or had been binding
One has or had been binding

We have or had been binding
You have or had been binding
They have or had been binding

Conditional (would, should or could)

I[1] would bind
You would bind
One would bind

We would bind
You would bind
They would bind

Conditional Progressive Tense

I would be binding
You would be binding
One would be binding

We would be binding
You would be binding
They would be binding

Conditional Perfect Tense

I would have bound
You would have bound
One would have bound

We would have bound
You would have bound
They would have bound

Conditional Perfect Progressive Tense

I would have been binding
You would have been binding
One would have been binding

We would have been binding
You would have been binding
They would have been binding

Subjunctive Present or Past Tense

I may or might bind
You may or might bind
One may or might bind

We may or might bind
You may or might bind
They may or might bind

Subjunctive Present or Past Perfect Tense

I may[2] or might have bound
You may or might have bound
One may or might have bound

We may or might have bound
You may or might have bound
They may or might have bound

Subjunctive Present or Past Perfect Progressive Tense

I may or might have been binding
You may or might have been binding
One may or might have been binding

We may or might have been binding
You may or might have been binding
They may or might have been binding

Imperative
(You) bind it.

---

[1] Often contracted: I'd, you'd, we'd, he'd, she'd, they'd.
[2] Subjunctive mood, p.1

Past Participles: bitten, bit

Indicative Present Tense   **BITE[1]**

I bite
You bite
One[2] bites

We bite
You bite
They bite

Past Tense

I bit
You bit
One bit

We bit
You bit
They bit

Future Tense

I[3] shall bite
You will bite
One will bite

We shall bite
You will bite
They will bite

Present or Past Progressive Tense

I[4] am or was biting
You are or were biting
One is or was biting

We are or were biting
You are or were biting
They are or were biting

Future Progressive Tense

I shall be biting
You will be biting
One will be biting

We shall be biting
You will be biting
They will be biting

Present or Past Perfect Tense

I[5] have or had bitten
You have or had bitten
One has or had bitten

We have or had bitten
You have or had bitten
They have or had bitten

Future Perfect Tense

I[3] shall have bitten
You will have bitten
One will have bitten

We shall have bitten
You will have bitten
They will have bitten

Future Perfect Progressive Tense

I shall have been biting
You will have been biting
One will have been biting

We shall have been biting
You will have been biting
They will have been biting

---

[1] Same conjugations for BACKBITE, FROSTBITE.
[2] Also she, he, it.
[3] Often contracted: I'll, you'll, he'll, she'll, we'll, or they'll (shall not: shan't, will not: won't).
[4] Often contracted: I'm, you're, we're, or they're.
[5] Often contracted: I've or I'd, you've or you'd, we've or we'd, or they've or they'd.

Present or Past Perfect Progressive Tense

I have or had been biting	We have or had been biting
You have or had been biting	You have or had been biting
One has or had been biting	They have or had been biting

Conditional (would, should or could)

I[1] would bite	We would bite
You would bite	You would bite
One would bite	They would bite

Conditional Progressive Tense

I would be biting	We would be biting
You would be biting	You would be biting
One would be biting	They would be biting

Conditional Perfect Tense

I would have bitten	We would have bitten
You would have bitten	You would have bitten
One would have bitten	They would have bitten

Conditional Perfect Progressive Tense

I would have been biting	We would have been biting
You would have been biting	You would have been biting
One would have been biting	They would have been biting

Subjunctive Present or Past Tense

I may or might bite	We may or might bite
You may or might bite	You may or might bite
One may or might bite	They may or might bite

Subjunctive Present or Past Perfect Tense

I may[2] or might have bitten	We may or might have bitten
You may or might have bitten	You may or might have bitten
One may or might have bitten	They may or might have bitten

Subjunctive Present or Past Perfect Progressive Tense

I may or might have been biting	We may or might have been biting
You may or might have been biting	You may or might have been biting
One may or might have been biting	They may or might have been biting

Imperative
(You) bite (it).

---

[1] Often contracted: I'd, you'd, we'd, he'd, she'd, they'd.
[2] Subjunctive mood, p.1

BLEED

Past Participle: bled

Indicative Present Tense

BLEED[1]

I bleed	We bleed
You bleed	You bleed
One[2] bleeds	They bleed

Past Tense

I bled	We bled
You bled	You bled
One bled	They bled

Future Tense

I[3] shall bleed	We shall bleed
You will bleed	You will bleed
One will bleed	They will bleed

Present or Past Progressive Tense

I[4] am or was bleeding	We are or were bleeding
You are or were bleeding	You are or were bleeding
One is or was bleeding	They are or were bleeding

Future Progressive Tense

I shall be bleeding	We shall be bleeding
You will be bleeding	You will be bleeding
One will be bleeding	They will be bleeding

Present or Past Perfect Tense

I[5] have or had bled	We have or had bled
You have or had bled	You have or had bled
One has or had bled	They have or had bled

Future Perfect Tense

I[3] shall have bled	We shall have bled
You will have bled	You will have bled
One will have bled	They will have bled

Future Perfect Progressive Tense

I shall have been bleeding	We shall have been bleeding
You will have been bleeding	You will have been bleeding
One will have been bleeding	They will have been bleeding

---

[1] Same conjugations for BREED, FEED, FLEE, INBREED, INTERBREED, LEAD, MEET, OVERFEED, PLEAD, (also regular), READ (Invariable but pronounced *red* for past and past participle, see appendix.), SLIDE (similar vowel change to *slid* but *progressive* form is *sliding*), SPEED, UNDERFEED

[2] Also she, he, it.

[3] Often contracted: I'll, you'll, he'll, she'll, we'll, or they'll (shall not: shan't, will not: won't).

[4] Often contracted: I'm, you're, we're, or they're.

[5] Often contracted: I've or I'd, you've or you'd, we've or we'd, or they've or they'd.

Present or Past Perfect Progressive Tense

I have or had been bleeding

You have or had been bleeding

One has or had been bleeding

We have or had been bleeding

You have or had been bleeding

They have or had been bleeding

Conditional (would, should or could)

I[1] would bleed

You would bleed

One would bleed

We would bleed

You would bleed

They would bleed

Conditional Progressive Tense

I would be bleeding

You would be bleeding

One would be bleeding

We would be bleeding

You would be bleeding

They would be bleeding

Conditional Perfect Tense

I would have bled

You would have bled

One would have bled

We would have bled

You would have bled

They would have bled

Conditional Perfect Progressive Tense

I would have been bleeding

You would have been bleeding

One would have been bleeding

We would have been bleeding

You would have been bleeding

They would have been bleeding

Subjunctive Present or Past Tense

I may or might bleed

You may or might bleed

One may or might bleed

We may or might bleed

You may or might bleed

They may or might bleed

Subjunctive Present or Past Perfect Tense

I may[2] or might have bled

You may or might have bled

One may or might have bled

We may or might have bled

You may or might have bled

They may or might have bled

Subjunctive Present or Past Perfect Progressive Tense

I may or might have been bleeding

You may or might have been bleeding

One may or might have been bleeding

We may or might have been bleeding

You may or might have been bleeding

They may or might have been bleeding

Imperative

(You) bleed (it).

---

[1] Often contracted: I'd, you'd, we'd, he'd, she'd, they'd.

[2] Subjunctive mood, p.1

BLOW

Past Participle: blown

Indicative Present Tense

I blow	We blow
You blow	You blow
One[2] blows	They blow

Past Tense

I blew	We blew
You blew	You blew
One blew	They blew

Future Tense

I[3] shall blow	We shall blow
You will blow	You will blow
One will blow	They will blow

Present or Past Progressive Tense

I[4] am or was blowing	We are or were blowing
You are or were blowing	You are or were blowing
One is or was blowing	They are or were blowing

Future Progressive Tense

I shall be blowing	We shall be blowing
You will be blowing	You will be blowing
One will be blowing	They will be blowing

Present or Past Perfect Tense

I[5] have or had blown	We have or had blown
You have or had blown	You have or had blown
One has or had blown	They have or had blown

Future Perfect Tense

I[3] shall have blown	We shall have blown
You will have blown	You will have blown
One will have blown	They will have blown

Future Perfect Progressive Tense

I shall have been blowing	We shall have been blowing
You will have been blowing	You will have been blowing
One will have been blowing	They will have been blowing

BLOW[1]

BREAK
(see SPEAK)

BREED
(see BLEED)

---

[1] Similar conjugations for DRAW, OUTDRAW, OVERDRAW (*p.p.* drawn); same for: GROW, KNOW, OUTGROW, OVERGROW, THROW.

[2] Also she, he, it.

[3] Often contracted: I'll, you'll, he'll, she'll, we'll, or they'll (shall not: shan't, will not: won't).

[4] Often contracted: I'm, you're, we're, or they're.

[5] Often contracted: I've or I'd, you've or you'd, we've or we'd, or they've or they'd.

Present or Past Perfect Progressive Tense

I have or had been blowing	We have or had been blowing
You have or had been blowing	You have or had been blowing
One has or had been blowing	They have or had been blowing

Conditional (would, should or could)

I[1] would blow	We would blow
You would blow	You would blow
One would blow	They would blow

Conditional Progressive Tense

I would be blowing	We would be blowing
You would be blowing	You would be blowing
One would be blowing	They would be blowing

Conditional Perfect Tense

I would have blown	We would have blown
You would have blown	You would have blown
One would have blown	They would have blown

Conditional Perfect Progressive Tense

I would have been blowing	We would have been blowing
You would have been blowing	You would have been blowing
One would have been blowing	They would have been blowing

Subjunctive Present or Past Tense

I may or might blow	We may or might blow
You may or might blow	You may or might blow
One may or might blow	They may or might blow

Subjunctive Present or Past Perfect Tense

I may[2] or might have blown	We may or might have blown
You may or might have blown	You may or might have blown
One may or might have blown	They may or might have blown

Subjunctive Present or Past Perfect Progressive Tense

I may or might have been blowing	We may or might have been blowing
You may or might have been blowing	You may or might have been blowing
One may or might have been blowing	They may or might have been blowing

Imperative
(You) blow it.

---

[1] Often contracted: I'd, you'd, we'd, he'd, she'd, they'd.
[2] Subjunctive mood, p.1

Past Participle: brought

Indicative Present Tense

I bring	We bring
You bring	You bring
One[2] brings	They bring

Past Tense

I brought	We brought
You brought	You brought
One brought	They brought

Future Tense

I[3] shall bring	We shall bring
You will bring	You will bring
One will bring	They will bring

Present or Past Progressive Tense

I[4] am or was bringing	We are or were bringing
You are or were bringing	You are or were bringing
One is or was bringing	They are or were bringing

Future Progressive Tense

I shall be bringing	We shall be bringing
You will be bringing	You will be bringing
One will be bringing	They will be bringing

Present or Past Perfect Tense

I[5] have or had brought	We have or had brought
You have or had brought	You have or had brought
One has or had brought	They have or had brought

Future Perfect Tense

I[3] shall have brought	We shall have brought
You will have brought	You will have brought
One will have brought	They will have brought

Future Perfect Progressive Tense

I shall have been bringing	We shall have been bringing
You will have been bringing	You will have been bringing
One will have been bringing	They will have been bringing

BRING[1]

BROADCAST
(invariable, see appendix)

---

[1] Similar conjugations for BESEECH (also regular), BUY, CATCH, FIGHT, SEEK, TEACH, THINK, WORK (*past and p.p., respectively, besought, bought, caught, fought, sought, taught, thought, wrought*).
[2] Also she, he, it.
[3] Often contracted: I'll, you'll, he'll, she'll, we'll, or they'll (shall not: shan't, will not: won't).
[4] Often contracted: I'm, you're, we're, or they're.
[5] Often contracted: I've or I'd, you've or you'd, we've or we'd, or they've or they'd.

Present or Past Perfect Progressive Tense

I have or had been bringing
You have or had been bringing
One has or had been bringing

We have or had been bringing
You have or had been bringing
They have or had been bringing

Conditional (would, should or could)

I[1] would bring
You would bring
One would bring

We would bring
You would bring
They would bring

Conditional Progressive Tense

I would be bringing
You would be bringing
One would be bringing

We would be bringing
You would be bringing
They would be bringing

Conditional Perfect Tense

I would have brought
You would have brought
One would have brought

We would have brought
You would have brought
They would have brought

Conditional Perfect Progressive Tense

I would have been bringing
You would have been bringing
One would have been bringing

We would have been bringing
You would have been bringing
They would have been bringing

Subjunctive Present or Past Tense

I may or might bring
You may or might bring
One may or might bring

We may or might bring
You may or might bring
They may or might bring

Subjunctive Present or Past Perfect Tense

I may[2] or might have brought
You may or might have brought
One may or might have brought

We may or might have brought
You may or might have brought
They may or might have brought

Subjunctive Present or Past Perfect Progressive Tense

I may or might have been bringing
You may or might have been bringing
One may or might have been bringing

We may or might have been bringing
You may or might have been bringing
They may or might have been bringing

Imperative
(You) bring it.

---

[1] Often contracted: I'd, you'd, we'd, he'd, she'd, they'd.
[2] Subjunctive mood, p.1

BUILD

Past Participle: built

BUILD[1]
(regular *t*
ending, see
appendix)

BURN
(regular:
see appendix)

BURST
(invariable,
also see appendix)

Indicative Present Tense

I build	We build
You build	You build
One[2] builds	They build

Past Tense

I built	We built
You built	You built
One built	They built

Future Tense

I[3] shall build	We shall build
You will build	You will build
One will build	They will build

Present or Past Progressive Tense

I[4] am or was building	We are or were building
You are or were building	You are or were building
One is or was building	They are or were building

Future Progressive Tense

I shall be building	We shall be building
You will be building	You will be building
One will be building	They will be building

Present or Past Perfect Tense

I[5] have or had built	We have or had built
You have or had built	You have or had built
One has or had built	They have or had built

Future Perfect Tense

I[3] shall have built	We shall have built
You will have built	You will have built
One will have built	They will have built

Future Perfect Progressive Tense

I shall have been building	We shall have been building
You will have been building	You will have been building
One will have been building	They will have been building

---

[1] Same conjugations for BEND, LEND, REND, SEND, SHEND (dial.), SPEND, WEND (archaic).
[2] Also she, he, it.
[3] Often contracted: I'll, you'll, he'll, she'll, we'll, or they'll (shall not: shan't, will not: won't).
[4] Often contracted: I'm, you're, we're, or they're.
[5] Often contracted: I've or I'd, you've or you'd, we've or we'd, or they've or they'd.

Present or Past Perfect Progressive Tense

I have or had been building
You have or had been building
One has or had been building

We have or had been building
You have or had been building
They have or had been building

Conditional (would, should or could)

I[1] would build
You would build
One would build

We would build
You would build
They would build

Conditional Progressive Tense

I would be building
You would be building
One would be building

We would be building
You would be building
They would be building

Conditional Perfect Tense

I would have built
You would have built
One would have built

We would have built
You would have built
They would have built

Conditional Perfect Progressive Tense

I would have been building
You would have been building
One would have been building

We would have been building
You would have been building
They would have been building

Subjunctive Present or Past Tense

I may or might build
You may or might build
One may or might build

We may or might build
You may or might build
They may or might build

Subjunctive Present or Past Perfect Tense

I may[2] or might have built
You may or might have built
One may or might have built

We may or might have built
You may or might have built
They may or might have built

Subjunctive Present or Past Perfect Progressive Tense

I may or might have been building
You may or might have been building
One may or might have been building

We may or might have been building
You may or might have been building
They may or might have been building

Imperative
(You) build it.

---

[1] Often contracted: I'd, you'd, we'd, he'd, she'd, they'd.
[2] Subjunctive mood, p.1

Past Participle: bought

Indicative Present Tense

I buy	We buy
You buy	You buy
One[2] buys	They buy

Past Tense

I bought	We bought
You bought	You bought
One bought	They bought

Future Tense

I[3] shall buy	We shall buy
You will buy	You will buy
One will buy	They will buy

Present or Past Progressive Tense

I[4] am or was buying	We are or were buying
You are or were buying	You are or were buying
One is or was buying	They are or were buying

Future Progressive Tense

I shall be buying	We shall be buying
You will be buying	You will be buying
One will be buying	They will be buying

Present or Past Perfect Tense

I[5] have or had bought	We have or had bought
You have or had bought	You have or had bought
One has or had bought	They have or had bought

Future Perfect Tense

I[3] shall have bought	We shall have bought
You will have bought	You will have bought
One will have bought	They will have bought

Future Perfect Progressive Tense

I shall have been buying	We shall have been buying
You will have been buying	You will have been buying
One will have been buying	They will have been buying

BUY[1]

CAN
(*past* could,
see auxiliaries)

CAST
(invariable, see
appendix)

---

[1] Similar conjugations for BESEECH (also regular), BRING, CATCH, FIGHT, SEEK, TEACH, THINK, WORK (*past and p.p., respectively, besought, brought, caught, fought, sought, taught, thought, wrought*).
[2] Also she, he, it.
[3] Often contracted: I'll, you'll, he'll, she'll, we'll, or they'll (shall not: shan't, will not: won't).
[4] Often contracted: I'm, you're, we're, or they're.
[5] Often contracted: I've or I'd, you've or you'd, we've or we'd, or they've or they'd.

Present or Past Perfect Progressive Tense

I have or had been buying
You have been buying
One has or had been buying

We have or had been buying
You have or had been buying
They have or had been buying

Conditional (would, should or could)

I[1] would buy
You would buy
One would buy

We would buy
You would buy
They would buy

Conditional Progressive Tense

I would be buying
You would be buying
One would be buying

We would be buying
You would be buying
They would be buying

Conditional Perfect Tense

I would have bought
You would have bought
One would have bought

We would have bought
You would have bought
They would have bought

Conditional Perfect Progressive Tense

I would have been buying
You would have been buying
One would have been buying

We would have been buying
You would have been buying
They would have been buying

Subjunctive Present or Past Tense

I may or might buy
You may or might buy
One may or might buy

We may or might buy
You may or might buy
They may or might buy

Subjunctive Present or Past Perfect Tense

I may[2] or might have bought
You may or might have bought
One may or might have bought

We may or might have bought
You may or might have bought
They may or might have bought

Subjunctive Present or Past Perfect Progressive Tense

I may or might have been buying
You may or might have been buying
One may or might have been buying

We may or might have been buying
You may or might have been buying
They may or might have been buying

Imperative: (You) buy it.

---

[1] Often contracted: I'd, you'd, we'd, he'd, she'd, they'd.
[2] Subjunctive mood, p.1

CATCH

Past Participle: caught

Indicative Present Tense

I catch	We catch
You catch	You catch
One[2] catches	They catch

Past Tense

I caught	We caught
You caught	You caught
One caught	They caught

Future Tense

I[3] shall catch	We shall catch
You will catch	You will catch
One will catch	They will catch

Present or Past Progressive Tense

I[4] am or was catching	We are or were catching
You are or were catching	You are or were catching
One is or was catching	They are or were catching

Future Progressive Tense

I shall be catching	We shall be catching
You will be catching	You will be catching
One will be catching	They will be catching

Present or Past Perfect Tense

I[5] have or had caught	We have or had caught
You have or had caught	You have or had caught
One has or had caught	They have or had caught

Future Perfect Tense

I[3] shall have caught	We shall have caught
You will have caught	You will have caught
One will have caught	They will have caught

Future Perfect Progressive Tense

I shall have been catching	We shall have been catching
You will have been catching	You will have been catching
One will have been catching	They will have been catching

CATCH[1]

CHIDE
(see HIDE)

CHOOSE
(past chose
p.p. chosen
progressive
choosing)

---

[1] Similar conjugations for BESEECH (also regular), BRING, BUY, FIGHT, SEEK, TEACH, THINK, WORK *(past and p.p., respectively, besought, brought, bought, fought, sought, taught, thought, wrought).*
[2] Also she, he, it.
[3] Often contracted: I'll, you'll, he'll, she'll, we'll, or they'll (shall not: shan't; will not: won't).
[4] Often contracted: I'm, you're, we're, or they're.
[5] Often contracted: I've or I'd, you've or you'd, we've or we'd, or they've or they'd.

Present or Past Perfect Progressive Tense

I have or had been catching
You have been catching
One has or had been catching

We have or had been catching
You have or had been catching
They have or had been catching

Conditional (would, should or could)

I[1] would catch
You would catch
One would catch

We would catch
You would catch
They would catch

Conditional Progressive Tense

I would be catching
You would be catching
One would be catching

We would be catching
You would be catching
They would be catching

Conditional Perfect Tense

I would have caught
You would have caught
One would have caught

We would have caught
You would have caught
They would have caught

Conditional Perfect Progressive Tense

I would have been catching
You would have been catching
One would have been catching

We would have been catching
You would have been catching
They would have been catching

Subjunctive Present or Past Tense

I may or might catch
You may or might catch
One may or might catch

We may or might catch
You may or might catch
They may or might catch

Subjunctive Present or Past Perfect Tense

I may[2] or might have caught
You may or might have caught
One may or might have caught

We may or might have caught
You may or might have caught
They may or might have caught

Subjunctive Present or Past Perfect Progressive Tense

I may or might have been catching
You may or might have been catching
One may or might have been catching

We may or might have been catching
You may or might have been catching
They may or might have been catching

Imperative: (You) catch (it).

---

[1] Often contracted: I'd, you'd, we'd, he'd, she'd, they'd.
[2] Subjunctive mood, p.1

CLEAVE

Past Participles: cloven, (split asunder) cleaved , cleft (to cling or sever), clave (archaic: to cling)

CLEAVE[1]
(also regular)

CLING
(see SWING)

CLOTHE
(also regular,
past and *p.p.* clad
progressive
clothing.)

Indicative Present Tense

I cleave	We cleave
You cleave	You cleave
One[2] cleaves	They cleave

Past Tense

I clove (or cleft)	We clove
You clove	You clove
One clove	They clove

Future Tense

I[3] shall cleave	We shall cleave
You will cleave	You will cleave
One will cleave	They will cleave

Present or Past Progressive Tense

I[4] am or was cleaving	We are or were cleaving
You are or were cleaving	You are or were cleaving
One is or was cleaving	They are or were cleaving

Future Progressive Tense

I shall be cleaving	We shall be cleaving
You will be cleaving	You will be cleaving
One will be cleaving	They will be cleaving

Present or Past Perfect Tense

I[5] have or had cloven	We have or had cloven
You have or had cloven	You have or had cloven
One has or had cloven	They have or had cloven

Future Perfect Tense

I[3] shall have cloven	We shall have cloven
You will have cloven	You will have cloven
One will have cloven	They will have cloven

Future Perfect Progressive Tense

I shall have been cleaving	We shall have been cleaving
You will have been cleaving	You will have been cleaving
One will have been cleaving	They will have been cleaving

---

[1] Similar conjugations for LEAVE (*past* and *p.p.* left only), HEAVE, WEAVE
[2] Also she, he, it.
[3] Often contracted: I'll, you'll, he'll, she'll, we'll, or they'll (shall not: shan't, will not: won't).
[4] Often contracted: I'm, you're, we're, or they're.
[5] Often contracted: I've or I'd, you've or you'd, we've or we'd, or they've or they'd.

Present or Past Perfect Progressive Tense

I have or had been cleaving
You have or had been cleaving
One has or had been cleaving

We have or had been cleaving
You have or had been cleaving
They have or had been cleaving

Conditional (would, should or could)

I[1] would cleave
You would cleave
One would cleave

We would cleave
You would cleave
They would cleave

Conditional Progressive Tense

I would be cleaving
You would be cleaving
One would be cleaving

We would be cleaving
You would be cleaving
They would be cleaving

Conditional Perfect Tense

I would have cloven
You would have cloven
One would have cloven

We would have cloven
You would have cloven
They would have cloven

Conditional Perfect Progressive Tense

I would have been cleaving
You would have been cleaving
One would have been cleaving

We would have been cleaving
You would have been cleaving
They would have been cleaving

Subjunctive Present or Past Tense

I may or might cleave
You may or might cleave
One may or might cleave

We may or might cleave
You may or might cleave
They may or might cleave

Subjunctive Present or Past Perfect Tense

I may[2] or might have cloven
You may or might have cloven
One may or might have cloven

We may or might have cloven
You may or might have cloven
They may or might have cloven

Subjunctive Present or Past Perfect Progressive Tense

I may or might have been cleaving
You may or might have been cleaving
One may or might have been cleaving

We may or might have been cleaving
You may or might have been cleaving
They may or might have been cleaving

Imperative

(You) cleave it.

---

[1] Often contracted: I'd, you'd, we'd, he'd, she'd, they'd.
[2] Subjunctive mood, p.1

Past Participle: come

Indicative Present Tense

I come	We come
You come	You come
One[2] comes	They come

Past Tense

I came	We came
You came	You came
One came	They came

Future Tense

I[3] shall come	We shall come
You will come	You will come
One will come	They will come

Present or Past Progressive Tense

I[4] am or was coming	We are or were coming
You are or were coming	You are or were coming
One is or was coming	They are or were coming

Future Progressive Tense

I shall be coming	We shall be coming
You will be coming	You will be coming
One will be coming	They will be coming

Present or Past Perfect Tense

I[5] have or had come	We have or had come
You have or had come	You have or had come
One has or had come	They have or had come

Future Perfect Tense

I[3] shall have come	We shall have come
You will have come	You will have come
One will have come	They will have come

Future Perfect Progressive Tense

I shall have been coming	We shall have been coming
You will have been coming	You will have been coming
One will have been coming	They will have been coming

COME[1]

COST
(see invariables)

COULD
(*past* of can,
see auxiliaries)

CREEP
(see SLEEP)

CRY
(see regular
"y" ending verb)

CUT
(see invariables)

DARE
(*past* and
p.p. durst
also regular)

DEAL
(see SPELL
for regular
t endings
in appendix)

DIG
(*past* and
p.p. dug
progressive
digging)

DIVE
(*past* dove
British:
regular only.)

---

[1] Similar conjugations for BECOME, RUN (differs for *progressive* running), FORERUN, OUTRUN, OVERRUN, OVERCOME.

[2] Also she, he, it.

[3] Often contracted: I'll, you'll, he'll, she'll, we'll, or they'll (shall not: shan't: will not: won't).

[4] Often contracted: I'm, you're, we're, or they're.

[5] Often contracted: I've or I'd, you've or you'd, we've or we'd, or they've or they'd.

Present or Past Perfect Progressive Tense

I have or had been coming
You have or had been coming
One has or had been coming

We have or had been coming
You have or had been coming
They have or had been coming

Conditional (would, should or could)

I[1] would come
You would come
One would come

We would come
You would come
They would come

Conditional Progressive Tense

I would be coming
You would be coming
One would be coming

We would be coming
You would be coming
They would be coming

Conditional Perfect Tense

I would have come
You would have come
One would have come

We would have come
You would have come
They would have come

Conditional Perfect Progressive Tense

I would have been coming
You would have been coming
One would have been coming

We would have been coming
You would have been coming
They would have been coming

Subjunctive Present or Past Tense

I may or might come
You may or might come
One may or might come

We may or might come
You may or might come
They may or might come

Subjunctive Present or Past Perfect Tense

I may[2] or might have come
You may or might have come
One may or might have come

We may or might have come
You may or might have come
They may or might have come

Subjunctive Present or Past Perfect Progressive Tense

I may or might have been coming
You may or might have been coming
One may or might have been coming

We may or might have been coming
You may or might have been coming
They may or might have been coming

Imperative
(You) come.

---

[1] Often contracted: I'd, you'd, we'd, he'd, she'd, they'd.
[2] Subjunctive mood, p.1

Past Participle: done

Indicative Present Tense

I do	We do
You do	You do
One[2] does	They do

Past Tense

I did	We did
You did	You did
One did	They did

Future Tense

I[3] shall do	We shall do
You will do	You will do
One will do	They will do

Present or Past Progressive Tense

I[4] am or was doing	We are or were doing
You are or were doing	You are or were doing
One is or was doing	They are or were doing

Future Progressive Tense

I shall be doing	We shall be doing
You will be doing	You will be doing
One will be doing	They will be doing

Present or Past Perfect Tense

I[5] have or had done	We have or had done
You have or had done	You have or had done
One has or had done	They have or had done

Future Perfect Tense

I[3] shall have done	We shall have done
You will have done	You will have done
One will have done	They will have done

Future Perfect Progressive Tense

I shall have been doing	We shall have been doing
You will have been doing	You will have been doing
One will have been doing	They will have been doing

DO[1]

Like *be* and *have, do* functions as an auxiliary as well as a main verb meaning to make, accomplish, instigate, or bring to pass, "They *do* that all the time."

(Also creates the emphatic voice, and command see p. 2)

DRAW
(see BLOW)

DREAM
(regular, see appendix)

DRINK
(see BEGIN, *past* drank, *p.p.* drunk *progressive* drinking)

---

[1] Same conjugations for OUTDO, REDO, UNDO.
[2] Also she, he, it.
[3] Often contracted: I'll, you'll, he'll, she'll, we'll, or they'll (shall not: shan't, will not: won't).
[4] Often contracted: I'm, you're, we're, or they're.
[5] Often contracted: I've or I'd, you've or you'd, we've or we'd, or they've or they'd.

Present or Past Perfect Progressive Tense

I have or had been doing
You have or had been doing
One has or had been doing

We have or had been doing
You have or had been doing
They have or had been doing

Conditional (would, should or could)

I[1] would do
You would do
One would do

We would do
You would do
They would do

Conditional Progressive Tense

I would be doing
You would be doing
One would be doing

We would be doing
You would be doing
They would be doing

Conditional Perfect Tense

I would have done
You would have done
One would have done

We would have done
You would have done
They would have done

Conditional Perfect Progressive Tense

I would have been doing
You would have been doing
One would have been doing

We would have been doing
You would have been doing
They would have been doing

Subjunctive Present or Past Tense

I may or might do
You may or might do
One may or might do

We may or might do
You may or might do
They may or might do

Subjunctive Present or Past Perfect Tense

I may[2] or might have done
You may or might have done
One may or might have done

We may or might have done
You may or might have done
They may or might have done

Subjunctive Present or Past Perfect Progressive Tense

I may or might have been doing
You may or might have been doing
One may or might have been doing

We may or might have been doing
You may or might have been doing
They may or might have been doing

Imperative
(You) do (it.)

---

[1] Often contracted: I'd, you'd, we'd, he'd, she'd, they'd.
[2] Subjunctive mood, p.1

DRIVE

Past Participle: driven

Indicative Present Tense

I drive	We drive
You drive	You drive
One[2] drives	They drive

Past Tense

I drove	We drove
You drove	You drove
One drove	They drove

Future Tense

I[3] shall drive	We shall drive
You will drive	You will drive
One will drive	They will drive

Present or Past Progressive Tense

I[4] am or was driving	We are or were driving
You are or were driving	You are or were driving
One is or was driving	They are or were driving

Future Progressive Tense

I shall be driving	We shall be driving
You will be driving	You will be driving
One will be driving	They will be driving

Present or Past Perfect Tense

I[5] have or had driven	We have or had driven
You have or had driven	You have or had driven
One has or had driven	They have or had driven

Future Perfect Tense

I[3] shall have driven	We shall have driven
You will have driven	You will have driven
One will have driven	They will have driven

Future Perfect Progressive Tense

I shall have been driving	We shall have been driving
You will have been driving	You will have been driving
One will have been driving	They will have been driving

DRIVE[1]

DWELL
*(past and p.p.
dwelt, also
regular)*

---

[1] Same or similar conjugations for ARISE, RIDE (*p.p.* ridden), RISE, STRIVE, THRIVE (also regular).
[2] Also she, he, it.
[3] Often contracted: I'll, you'll, he'll, she'll, we'll, or they'll (shall not: shan't, will not: won't).
[4] Often contracted: I'm, you're, we're, or they're.
[5] Often contracted: I've or I'd, you've or you'd, we've or we'd, or they've or they'd.

Present or Past Perfect Progressive Tense

I have or had been driving
You have or had been driving
One has or had been driving

We have or had been driving
You have or had been driving
They have or had been driving

Conditional (would, should or could)

I[1] would drive
You would drive
One would drive

We would drive
You would drive
They would drive

Conditional Progressive Tense

I would be driving
You would be driving
One would be driving

We would be driving
You would be driving
They would be driving

Conditional Perfect Tense

I would have driven
You would have driven
One would have driven

We would have driven
You would have driven
They would have driven

Conditional Perfect Progressive Tense

I would have been driving
You would have been driving
One would have been driving

We would have been driving
You would have been driving
They would have been driving

Subjunctive Present or Past Tense

I may or might drive
You may or might drive
One may or might drive

We may or might drive
You may or might drive
They may or might drive

Subjunctive Present or Past Perfect Tense

I may[2] or might have driven
You may or might have driven
One may or might have driven

We may or might have driven
You may or might have driven
They may or might have driven

Subjunctive Present or Past Perfect Progressive Tense

I may or might have been driving
You may or might have been driving
One may or might have been driving

We may or might have been driving
You may or might have been driving
They may or might have been driving

Imperative
(You) drive (it).

---

[1] Often contracted: I'd, you'd, we'd, he'd, she'd, they'd.
[2] Subjunctive mood, p.1

EAT

Past Participle: eaten

Indicative Present Tense

EAT[1]

ENGRAVE
(mainly regular
see MOW
for British *p.p.*)

I eat	We eat
You eat	You eat
One[2] eats	They eat

Past Tense

I ate	We ate
You ate	You ate
One ate	They ate

Future Tense

I[3] shall eat	We shall eat
You will eat	You will eat
One will eat	They will eat

Present or Past Progressive Tense

I[4] am or was eating	We are or were eating
You are or were eating	You are or were eating
One is or was eating	They are or were eating

Future Progressive Tense

I shall be eating	We shall be eating
You will be eating	You will be eating
One will be eating	They will be eating

Present or Past Perfect Tense

I[5] have or had eaten	We have or had eaten
You have or had eaten	You have or had eaten
One has or had eaten	They have or had eaten

Future Perfect Tense

I[3] shall have eaten	We shall have eaten
You will have eaten	You will have eaten
One will have eaten	They will have eaten

Future Perfect Progressive Tense

I shall have been eating	We shall have been eating
You will have been eating	You will have been eating
One will have been eating	They will have been eating

---

[1] Same conjugations for OVEREAT, UNDEREAT.
[2] Also she, he, it.
[3] Often contracted: I'll, you'll, he'll, she'll, we'll, or they'll (shall not: shan't, will not: won't).
[4] Often contracted: I'm, you're, we're, or they're.
[5] Often contracted: I've or I'd, you've or you'd, we've or we'd, or they've or they'd.

Present or Past Perfect Progressive Tense

I have or had been eating	We have or had been eating
You have or had been eating	You have or had been eating
One has or had been eating	They have or had been eating

Conditional (would, should or could)

I[1] would eat	We would eat
You would eat	You would eat
One would eat	They would eat

Conditional Progressive Tense

I would be eating	We would be eating
You would be eating	You would be eating
One would be eating	They would be eating

Conditional Perfect Tense

I would have eaten	We would have eaten
You would have eaten	You would have eaten
One would have eaten	They would have eaten

Conditional Perfect Progressive Tense

I would have been eating	We would have been eating
You would have been eating	You would have been eating
One would have been eating	They would have been eating

Subjunctive Present or Past Tense

I may or might eat	We may or might eat
You may or might eat	You may or might eat
One may or might eat	They may or might eat

Subjunctive Present or Past Perfect Tense

I may[2] or might have eaten	We may or might have eaten
You may or might have eaten	You may or might have eaten
One may or might have eaten	They may or might have eaten

Subjunctive Present or Past Perfect Progressive Tense

I may or might have been eating	We may or might have been eating
You may or might have been eating	You may or might have been eating
One may or might have been eating	They may or might have been eating

Imperative
(You) eat (it.)

---

[1] Often contracted: I'd, you'd, we'd, he'd, she'd, they'd.
[2] Subjunctive mood, p.1

FALL

Past Participle: fallen

Indicative Present Tense

I fall	We fall
You fall	You fall
One[2] falls	They fall

Past Tense

I fell	We fell
You fell	You fell
One fell	They fell

Future Tense

I[3] shall fall	We shall fall
You will fall	You will fall
One will fall	They will fall

Present or Past Progressive Tense

I[4] am or was falling	We are or were falling
You are or were falling	You are or were falling
One is or was falling	They are or were falling

Future Progressive Tense

I shall be falling	We shall be falling
You will be falling	You will be falling
One will be falling	They will be falling

Present or Past Perfect Tense

I[5] have or had fallen	We have or had fallen
You have or had fallen	You have or had fallen
One has or had fallen	They have or had fallen

Future Perfect Tense

I[3] shall have fallen	We shall have fallen
You will have fallen	You will have fallen
One will have fallen	They will have fallen

Future Perfect Progressive Tense

I shall have been falling	We shall have been falling
You will have been falling	You will have been falling
One will have been falling	They will have been falling

---

[1] Same conjugations for BEFALL.
[2] Also she, he, it.
[3] Often contracted: I'll, you'll, he'll, she'll, we'll, or they'll (shall not: shan't, will not: won't).
[4] Often contracted: I'm, you're, we're, or they're.
[5] Often contracted: I've or I'd, you've or you'd, we've or we'd, or they've or they'd.

FALL[1]

FEED
(see BLEED)

FEEL
(linking, transitive and intransitive verb, see appendix)

FIGHT
(see BRING)

FIND
(see BIND)

FIT
(see invariables)

FLEE
(see BLEED)

FLING
(see SWING)

FLY
(see BLOW, note "y" verb in appendix)

FORBEAR
(see BEAR)

FORBID
(see BID)

FORCEFEED
(see BLEED)

FORECAST
(see invariables)

FOREDO
(see DO)

Present or Past Perfect Progressive Tense

I have or had been falling
You have or had been falling
One has or had been falling

We have or had been falling
You have or had been falling
They have or had been falling

Conditional (would, should or could)

I[1] would fall
You would fall
One would fall

We would fall
You would fall
They would fall

Conditional Progressive Tense

I would be falling
You would be falling
One would be falling

We would be falling
You would be falling
They would be falling

Conditional Perfect Tense

I would have fallen
You would have fallen
One would have fallen

We would have fallen
You would have fallen
They would have fallen

Conditional Perfect Progressive Tense

I would have been falling
You would have been falling
One would have been falling

We would have been falling
You would have been falling
They would have been falling

Subjunctive Present or Past Tense

I may or might fall
You may or might fall
One may or might fall

We may or might fall
You may or might fall
They may or might fall

Subjunctive Present or Past Perfect Tense

I may[2] or might have fallen
You may or might have fallen
One may or might have fallen

We may or might have fallen
You may or might have fallen
They may or might have fallen

Subjunctive Present or Past Perfect Progressive Tense

I may or might have been falling
You may or might have been falling
One may or might have been falling

We may or might have been falling
You may or might have been falling
They may or might have been falling

Imperative
(You) fall.

---

[1] Often contracted: I'd, you'd, we'd, he'd, she'd, they'd.
[2] Subjunctive mood, p.1

FOREFEEL
(see FEEL)

FOREGO
(see GO)

FOREKNOW
(see BLOW)

FORERUN
(see RUN)

FORESEE
(see SEE)

FORGET
(see GET)

FORGIVE
(see GIVE)

FORSAKE
(past forsook
p.p. forsaken
also regular)

FORESWEAR
(see BEAR)

FORETELL
(see SELL)

FREEZE

Past Participlte: frozen

Indicative Present Tense

I freeze
You freeze
One[2] freezes

We freeze
You freeze
They freeze

Past Tense

I froze
You froze
One froze

We froze
You froze
They froze

Future Tense

I[3] shall freeze
You will freeze
One will freeze

We shall freeze
You will freeze
They will freeze

Present or Past Progressive Tense

I[4] am or was freezing
You are or were freezing
One is or was freezing

We are or were freezing
You are or were freezing
They are or were freezing

Future Progressive Tense

I shall be freezing
You will be freezing
One will be freezing

We shall be freezing
You will be freezing
They will be freezing

Present or Past Perfect Tense

I[5] have or had frozen
You have or had frozen
One has or had frozen

We have or had frozen
You have or had frozen
They have or had frozen

Future Perfect Tense

I[3] shall have frozen
You will have frozen
One will have frozen

We shall have frozen
You will have frozen
They will have frozen

Future Perfect Progressive Tense

I shall have been freezing
You will have been freezing
One will have been freezing

We shall have been freezing
You will have been freezing
They will have been freezing

FREEZE[1]

FROSTBITE
(see BITE)

GAINSAY
(see SAY)

GELD
(regular:
see SPELL
in appendix)

---

[1] Same conjugations for QUICK-FREEZE, REFREEZE.
[2] Also she, he, it.
[3] Often contracted: I'll, you'll, he'll, she'll, we'll, or they'll (shall not: shan't, will not: won't).
[4] Often contracted: I'm, you're, we're, or they're.
[5] Often contracted: I've or I'd, you've or you'd, we've or we'd, or they've or they'd.

Present or Past Perfect Progressive Tense

I have or had been freezing	We have or had been freezing
You have or had been freezing	You have or had been freezing
One has or had been freezing	They have or had been freezing

Conditional (would, should or could)

I[1] would freeze	We would freeze
You would freeze	You would freeze
One would freeze	They would freeze

Conditional Progressive Tense

I would be freezing	We would be freezing
You would be freezing	You would be freezing
One would be freezing	They would be freezing

Conditional Perfect Tense

I would have frozen	We would have frozen
You would have frozen	You would have frozen
One would have frozen	They would have frozen

Conditional Perfect Progressive Tense

I would have been freezing	We would have been freezing
You would have been freezing	You would have been freezing
One would have been freezing	They would have been freezing

Subjunctive Present or Past Tense

I may or might freeze	We may or might freeze
You may or might freeze	You may or might freeze
One may or might freeze	They may or might freeze

Subjunctive Present or Past Perfect Tense

I may[2] or might have frozen	We may or might have frozen
You may or might have frozen	You may or might have frozen
One may or might have frozen	They may or might have frozen

Subjunctive Present or Past Perfect Progressive Tense

I may or might have been freezing	We may or might have been freezing
You may or might have been freezing	You may or might have been freezing
One may or might have been freezing	They may or might have been freezing

Imperative
(You) freeze it.

---

[1] Often contracted: I'd, you'd, we'd, he'd, she'd, they'd.
[2] Subjunctive mood, p.1

Past Participles: got (also British), gotten

Indicative Present Tense   **GET[1]**

I get	We get
You get	You get
One[2] gets	They get

GILD
(regular:
see SPELL
in appendix)

Past Tense

I got	We got
You got	You got
One got	They got

GIRD
(regular:
see SPELL
in appendix)

Future Tense

I[3] shall get	We shall get
You will get	You will get
One will get	They will get

Present or Past Progressive Tense

I[4] am or was getting	We are or were getting
You are or were getting	You are or were getting
One is or was getting	They are or were getting

Future Progressive Tense

I shall be getting	We shall be getting
You will be getting	You will be getting
One will be getting	They will be getting

Present or Past Perfect Tense

I[5] have or had got	We have or had got
You have or had got	You have or had got
One has or had got	They have or had got

Future Perfect Tense

I[3] shall have got	We shall have got
You will have got	You will have got
One will have got	They will have got

Future Perfect Progressive Tense

I shall have been getting	We shall have been getting
You will have been getting	You will have been getting
One will have been getting	They will have been getting

---

[1] Same conjugations for FORGET (*p.p. forgotten*).
[2] Also she, he, it.
[3] Often contracted: I'll, you'll, he'll, she'll, we'll, or they'll (shall not: shan't, will not: won't).
[4] Often contracted: I'm, you're, we're, or they're.
[5] Often contracted: I've or I'd, you've or you'd, we've or we'd, or they've or they'd.

Present or Past Perfect Progressive Tense

I have or had been getting	We have or had been getting
You have or had been getting	You have or had been getting
One has or had been getting	They have or had been getting

Conditional (would, should or could)

I[1] would get	We would get
You would get	You would get
One would get	They would get

Conditional Progressive Tense

I would be getting	We would be getting
You would be getting	You would be getting
One would be getting	They would be getting

Conditional Perfect Tense

I would have got	We would have got
You would have got	You would have got
One would have got	They would have got

Conditional Perfect Progressive Tense

I would have been getting	We would have been getting
You would have been getting	You would have been getting
One would have been getting	They would have been getting

Subjunctive Present or Past Tense

I may or might get	We may or might get
You may or might get	You may or might get
One may or might get	They may or might get

Subjunctive Present or Past Perfect Tense

I may[2] or might have got	We may or might have got
You may or might have got	You may or might have got
One may or might have got	They may or might have got

Subjunctive Present or Past Perfect Progressive Tense

I may or might have been getting	We may or might have been getting
You may or might have been getting	You may or might have been getting
One may or might have been getting	They may or might have been getting

Imperative
(You) get it.

---

[1] Often contracted: I'd, you'd, we'd, he'd, she'd, they'd.
[2] Subjunctive mood, p.1

GIVE

Past Participle: given

Indicative Present Tense

GIVE[1]

I give
You give
One[2] gives

We give
You give
They give

Past Tense

I gave
You gave
One gave

We gave
You gave
They gave

Future Tense

I[3] shall give
You will give
One will give

We shall give
You will give
They will give

Present or Past Progressive Tense

I[4] am or was giving
You are or were giving
One is or was giving

We are or were giving
You are or were giving
They are or were giving

Future Progressive Tense

I shall be giving
You will be giving
One will be giving

We shall be giving
You will be giving
They will be giving

Present or Past Perfect Tense

I[5] have or had given
You have or had given
One has or had given

We have or had given
You have or had given
They have or had given

Future Perfect Tense

I[3] shall have given
You will have given
One will have given

We shall have given
You will have given
They will have given

Future Perfect Progressive Tense

I shall have been giving
You will have been giving
One will have been giving

We shall have been giving
You will have been giving
They will have been giving

---

[1] Same conjugations for FORGIVE.
[2] Also she, he, it.
[3] Often contracted: I'll, you'll, he'll, she'll, we'll, or they'll (shall not: shan't, will not: won't).
[4] Often contracted: I'm, you're, we're, or they're.
[5] Often contracted: I've or I'd, you've or you'd, we've or we'd, or they've or they'd.

Present or Past Perfect Progressive Tense

I have or had been giving	We have or had been giving
You have or had been giving	You have or had been giving
One has or had been giving	They have or had been giving

Conditional (would, should or could)

I[1] would give	We would give
You would give	You would give
One would give	They would give

Conditional Progressive Tense

I would be giving	We would be giving
You would be giving	You would be giving
One would be giving	They would be giving

Conditional Perfect Tense

I would have given	We would have given
You would have given	You would have given
One would have given	They would have given

Conditional Perfect Progressive Tense

I would have been giving	We would have been giving
You would have been giving	You would have been giving
One would have been giving	They would have been giving

Subjunctive Present or Past Tense

I may or might give	We may or might give
You may or might give	You may or might give
One may or might give	They may or might give

Subjunctive Present or Past Perfect Tense

I may[2] or might have given	We may or might have given
You may or might have given	You may or might have given
One may or might have given	They may or might have given

Subjunctive Present or Past Perfect Progressive Tense

I may or might have been giving	We may or might have been giving
You may or might have been giving	You may or might have been giving
One may or might have been giving	They may or might have been giving

Imperative
(You) give it.

---

[1] Often contracted: I'd, you'd, we'd, he'd, she'd, they'd.
[2] Subjunctive mood, p.1

Past Participle: gone

Indicative Present Tense

		GO[1]
I go	We go	
You go	You go	**GRAVE**
One[2] goes	They go	(see MOW)

Past Tense

		GRIND
I went	We went	(see BIND)
You went	You went	
One went	They went	**GROW**
		(see BLOW)

Future Tense

I[3] shall go   We shall go
You will go   You will go
One will go   They will go

Present or Past Progressive Tense

I[4] am or was going   We are or were going
You are or were going   You are or were going
One is or was going   They are or were going

Future Progressive Tense

I shall be going   We shall be going
You will be going   You will be going
One will be going   They will be going

Present or Past Perfect Tense

I[5] have or had gone   We have or had gone
You have or had gone   You have or had gone
One has or had gone   They have or had gone

Future Perfect Tense

I[3] shall have gone   We shall have gone
You will have gone   You will have gone
One will have gone   They will have gone

Future Perfect Progressive Tense

I shall have been going   We shall have been going
You will have been going   You will have been going
One will have been going   They will have been going

---

[1] Same conjugations for FOREGO, UNDERGO.
[2] Also she, he, it.
[3] Often contracted: I'll, you'll, he'll, she'll, we'll, or they'll (shall not: shan't, will not: won't).
[4] Often contracted: I'm, you're, we're, or they're.
[5] Often contracted: I've or I'd, you've or you'd, we've or we'd, or they've or they'd.

Present or Past Perfect Progressive Tense

I have or had been going

You have or had been going

One has or had been going

We have or had been going

You have or had been going

They have or had been going

Conditional (would, should or could)

I[1] would go

You would go

One would go

We would go

You would go

They would go

Conditional Progressive Tense

I would be going

You would be going

One would be going

We would be going

You would be going

They would be going

Conditional Perfect Tense

I would have gone

You would have gone

One would have gone

We would have gone

You would have gone

They would have gone

Conditional Perfect Progressive Tense

I would have been going

You would have been going

One would have been going

We would have been going

You would have been going

They would have been going

Subjunctive Present or Past Tense

I may or might go

You may or might go

One may or might go

We may or might go

You may or might go

They may or might go

Subjunctive Present or Past Perfect Tense

I may[2] or might have gone

You may or might have gone

One may or might have gone

We may or might have gone

You may or might have gone

They may or might have gone

Subjunctive Present or Past Perfect Progressive Tense

I may or might have been going

You may or might have been going

One may or might have been going

We may or might have been going

You may or might have been going

They may or might have been going

Imperative

(You) go

---

[1] Often contracted: I'd, you'd, we'd, he'd, she'd, they'd.

[2] Subjunctive mood, p.1

HANG

Past Participles: hung (clothes); hanged (executions)

Indicative Present Tense

I hang	We hang
You hang	You hang
One[2] hangs	They hang

Past Tense

I hung	We hung
You hung	You hung
One hung	They hung

Future Tense

I[3] shall hang	We shall hang
You will hang	You will hang
One will hang	They will hang

Present or Past Progressive Tense

I[4] am or was hanging	We are or were hanging
You are or were hanging	You are or were hanging
One is or was hanging	They are or were hanging

Future Progressive Tense

I shall be hanging	We shall be hanging
You will be hanging	You will be hanging
One will be hanging	They will be hanging

Present or Past Perfect Tense

I[5] have or had hung	We have or had hung
You have or had hung	You have or had hung
One has or had hung	They have or had hung

Future Perfect Tense

I[3] shall have hung	We shall have hung
You will have hung	You will have hung
One will have hung	They will have hung

Future Perfect Progressive Tense

I shall have been hanging	We shall have been hanging
You will have been hanging	You will have been hanging
One will have been hanging	They will have been hanging

HANG[1]
(also regular)

HAVE
(as an
auxiliary, p.2
past and
p.p. had,
progressive
having.)

---

[1] Same conjugations for FLING, OVERHANG, SLING, STRING (also regular for instruments), SWING, WRING.

[2] Also she, he, it.

[3] Often contracted: I'll, you'll, he'll, she'll, we'll, or they'll (shall not: shan't, will not: won't).

[4] Often contracted: I'm, you're, we're, or they're.

[5] Often contracted: I've or I'd, you've or you'd, we've or we'd, or they've or they'd.

Present or Past Perfect Progressive Tense

I have or had been hanging
You have or had been hanging
One has or had been hanging

We have or had been hanging
You have or had been hanging
They have or had been hanging

Conditional (would, should or could)

I[1] would hang
You would hang
One would hang

We would hang
You would hang
They would hang

Conditional Progressive Tense

I would be hanging
You would be hanging
One would be hanging

We would be hanging
You would be hanging
They would be hanging

Conditional Perfect Tense

I would have hung
You would have hung
One would have hung

We would have hung
You would have hung
They would have hung

Conditional Perfect Progressive Tense

I would have been hanging
You would have been hanging
One would have been hanging

We would have been hanging
You would have been hanging
They would have been hanging

Subjunctive Present or Past Tense

I may or might hang
You may or might hang
One may or might hang

We may or might hang
You may or might hang
They may or might hang

Subjunctive Present or Past Perfect Tense

I may[2] or might have hung
You may or might have hung
One may or might have hung

We may or might have hung
You may or might have hung
They may or might have hung

Subjunctive Present or Past Perfect Progressive Tense

I may or might have been hanging
You may or might have been hanging
One may or might have been hanging

We may or might have been hanging
You may or might have been hanging
They may or might have been hanging

Imperative
(You) hang (it.)

---

[1] Often contracted: I'd, you'd, we'd, he'd, she'd, they'd.
[2] Subjunctive mood, p.1

Past Participle: heard

Indicative Present Tense

HEAR[1]

I hear	We hear
You hear	You hear
One[2] hears	They hear

Past Tense

I heard	We heard
You heard	You heard
One heard	They heard

Future Tense

I[3] shall hear	We shall hear
You will hear	You will hear
One will hear	They will hear

Present or Past Progressive Tense

I[4] am or was hearing	We are or were hearing
You are or were hearing	You are or were hearing
One is or was hearing	They are or were hearing

Future Progressive Tense

I shall be hearing	We shall be hearing
You will be hearing	You will be hearing
One will be hearing	They will be hearing

Present or Past Perfect Tense

I[5] have or had heard	We have or had heard
You have or had heard	You have or had heard
One has or had heard	They have or had heard

Future Perfect Tense

I[3] shall have heard	We shall have heard
You will have heard	You will have heard
One will have heard	They will have heard

Future Perfect Progressive Tense

I shall have been hearing	We shall have been hearing
You will have been hearing	You will have been hearing
One will have been hearing	They will have been hearing

---

[1] Same conjugations for MISHEAR, OVERHEAR, REHEAR.
[2] Also she, he, it.
[3] Often contracted: I'll, you'll, he'll, she'll, we'll, or they'll (shall not: shan't, will not: won't).
[4] Often contracted: I'm, you're, we're, or they're.
[5] Often contracted: I've or I'd, you've or you'd, we've or we'd, or they've or they'd.

Present or Past Perfect Progressive Tense

I have or had been hearing
You have or had been hearing
One has or had been hearing

We have or had been hearing
You have or had been hearing
They have or had been hearing

Conditional (would, should or could)

I[1] would hear
You would hear
One would hear

We would hear
You would hear
They would hear

Conditional Progressive Tense

I would be hearing
You would be hearing
One would be hearing

We would be hearing
You would be hearing
They would be hearing

Conditional Perfect Tense

I would have heard
You would have heard
One would have heard

We would have heard
You would have heard
They would have heard

Conditional Perfect Progressive Tense

I would have been hearing
You would have been hearing
One would have been hearing

We would have been hearing
You would have been hearing
They would have been hearing

Subjunctive Present or Past Tense

I may or might hear
You may or might hear
One may or might hear

We may or might hear
You may or might hear
They may or might hear

Subjunctive Present or Past Perfect Tense

I may[2] or might have heard
You may or might have heard
One may or might have heard

We may or might have heard
You may or might have heard
They may or might have heard

Subjunctive Present or Past Perfect Progressive Tense

I may or might have been hearing
You may or might have been hearing
One may or might have been hearing

We may or might have been hearing
You may or might have been hearing
They may or might have been hearing

Imperative
(You) hear it.

---

[1] Often contracted: I'd, you'd, we'd, he'd, she'd, they'd.
[2] Subjunctive mood, p.1

HEAVE

Past Participles: hoven, heaved, hove

HEAVE[1]
(also regular)

HEW
(see MOW)

Indicative Present Tense

I heave	We heave
You heave	You heave
One[2] heaves	They heave

Past Tense

I hove	We hove
You hove	You hove
One hove	They hove

Future Tense

I[3] shall heave	We shall heave
You will heave	You will heave
One will heave	They will heave

Present or Past Progressive Tense

I[4] am or was heaving	We are or were heaving
You are or were heaving	You are or were heaving
One is or was heaving	They are or were heaving

Future Progressive Tense

I shall be heaving	We shall be heaving
You will be heaving	You will be heaving
One will be heaving	They will be heaving

Present or Past Perfect Tense

I[5] have or had hoven	We have or had hoven
You have or had hoven	You have or had hoven
One has or had hoven	They have or had hoven

Future Perfect Tense

I[3] shall have hoven	We shall have hoven
You will have hoven	You will have hoven
One will have hoven	They will have hoven

Future Perfect Progressive Tense

I shall have been heaving	We shall have been heaving
You will have been heaving	You will have been heaving
One will have been heaving	They will have been heaving

---

[1] Same conjugations for CLEAVE (also regular, *clave*: archaic, American), WEAVE (rarely regular).
[2] Also she, he, it.
[3] Often contracted: I'll, you'll, he'll, she'll, we'll, or they'll (shall not: shan't, will not: won't).
[4] Often contracted: I'm, you're, we're, or they're.
[5] Often contracted: I've or I'd, you've or you'd, we've or we'd, or they've or they'd.

Present or Past Perfect Progressive Tense

I have or had been heaving	We have or had been heaving
You have or had been heaving	You have or had been heaving
One has or had been heaving	They have or had been heaving

Conditional (would, should or could)

I[1] would heave	We would heave
You would heave	You would heave
One would heave	They would heave

Conditional Progressive Tense

I would be heaving	We would be heaving
You would be heaving	You would be heaving
One would be heaving	They would be heaving

Conditional Perfect Tense

I would have hoven	We would have hoven
You would have hoven	You would have hoven
One would have hoven	They would have hoven

Conditional Perfect Progressive Tense

I would have been heaving	We would have been heaving
You would have been heaving	You would have been heaving
One would have been heaving	They would have been heaving

Subjunctive Present or Past Tense

I may or might heave	We may or might heave
You may or might heave	You may or might heave
One may or might heave	They may or might heave

Subjunctive Present or Past Perfect Tense

I may[2] or might have hoven	We may or might have hoven
You may or might have hoven	You may or might have hoven
One may or might have hoven	They may or might have hoven

Subjunctive Present or Past Perfect Progressive Tense

I may or might have been heaving	We may or might have been heaving
You may or might have been heaving	You may or might have been heaving
One may or might have been heaving	They may or might have been heaving

Imperative
(You) heave it.

---

[1] Often contracted: I'd, you'd, we'd, he'd, she'd, they'd.
[2] Subjunctive mood, p.1

HIDE

Past Participles: hidden, hid

Indicative Present Tense

HIDE[1]

I hide	We hide
You hide	You hide
One[2] hides	They hide

Past Tense

I hid	We hid
You hid	You hid
One hid	They hid

Future Tense

I[3] shall hide	We shall hide
You will hide	You will hide
One will hide	They will hide

Present or Past Progressive Tense

I[4] am or was hiding	We are or were hiding
You are or were hiding	You are or were hiding
One is or was hiding	They are or were hiding

Future Progressive Tense

I shall be hiding	We shall be hiding
You will be hiding	You will be hiding
One will be hiding	They will be hiding

Present or Past Perfect Tense

I[5] have or had hidden	We have or had hidden
You have or had hidden	You have or had hidden
One has or had hidden	They have or had hidden

Future Perfect Tense

I[3] shall have hidden	We shall have hidden
You will have hidden	You will have hidden
One will have hidden	They will have hidden

Future Perfect Progressive Tense

I shall have been hiding	We shall have been hiding
You will have been hiding	You will have been hiding
One will have been hiding	They will have been hiding

---

[1] Same conjugations for CHIDE, BID (also invariable).
[2] Also she, he, it.
[3] Often contracted: I'll, you'll, he'll, she'll, we'll, or they'll (shall not: shan't, will not: won't).
[4] Often contracted: I'm, you're, we're, or they're.
[5] Often contracted: I've or I'd, you've or you'd, we've or we'd, or they've or they'd.

Present or Past Perfect Progressive Tense

I have or had been hiding	We have or had been hiding
You have or had been hiding	You have or had been hiding
One has or had been hiding	They have or had been hiding

Conditional (would, should or could)

I[1] would hide	We would hide
You would hide	You would hide
One would hide	They would hide

Conditional Progressive Tense

I would be hiding	We would be hiding
You would be hiding	You would be hiding
One would be hiding	They would be hiding

Conditional Perfect Tense

I would have hidden	We would have hidden
You would have hidden	You would have hidden
One would have hidden	They would have hidden

Conditional Perfect Progressive Tense

I would have been hiding	We would have been hiding
You would have been hiding	You would have been hiding
One would have been hiding	They would have been hiding

Subjunctive Present or Past Tense

I may or might hide	We may or might hide
You may or might hide	You may or might hide
One may or might hide	They may or might hide

Subjunctive Present or Past Perfect Tense

I may[2] or might have hidden	We may or might have hidden
You may or might have hidden	You may or might have hidden
One may or might have hidden	They may or might have hidden

Subjunctive Present or Past Perfect Progressive Tense

I may or might have been hiding	We may or might have been hiding
You may or might have been hiding	You may or might have been hiding
One may or might have been hiding	They may or might have been hiding

Imperative
(You) hide (it).

---

[1] Often contracted: I'd, you'd, we'd, he'd, she'd, they'd.
[2] Subjunctive mood, p.1

HOLD

Past Participle: held

Indicative Present Tense

I hold	We hold
You hold	You hold
One[2] holds	They hold

Past Tense

I held	We held
You held	You held
One held	They held

Future Tense

I[3] shall hold	We shall hold
You will hold	You will hold
One will hold	They will hold

Present or Past Progressive Tense

I[4] am or was holding	We are or were holding
You are or were holding	You are or were holding
One is or was holding	They are or were holding

Future Progressive Tense

I shall be holding	We shall be holding
You will be holding	You will be holding
One will be holding	They will be holding

Present or Past Perfect Tense

I[5] have or had held	We have or had held
You have or had held	You have or had held
One has or had held	They have or had held

Future Perfect Tense

I[3] shall have held	We shall have held
You will have held	You will have held
One will have held	They will have held

Future Perfect Progressive Tense

I shall have been holding	We shall have been holding
You will have been holding	You will have been holding
One will have been holding	They will have been holding

HOLD[1]

HURT
(see invariables)

INBREED
(see BLEED)

INTERBREED
(see BLEED)

KEEP
(see SLEEP)

KNEEL
(*past* and *p.p.* knelt
progressive kneeling)

KNIT
(see invariables)

KNOW
(see BLOW)

LADE
(see MOW)

---

[1] Same conjugations for BEHOLD, UPHOLD, WITHHOLD.
[2] Also she, he, it.
[3] Often contracted: I'll, you'll, he'll, she'll, we'll, or they'll (shall not: shan't, will not: won't).
[4] Often contracted: I'm, you're, we're, or they're.
[5] Often contracted: I've or I'd, you've or you'd, we've or we'd, or they've or they'd.

Present or Past Perfect Progressive Tense

I have or had been holding
You have or had been holding
One has or had been holding

We have or had been holding
You have or had been holding
They have or had been holding

Conditional (would, should or could)

I[1] would hold
You would hold
One would hold

We would hold
You would hold
They would hold

Conditional Progressive Tense

I would be holding
You would be holding
One would be holding

We would be holding
You would be holding
They would be holding

Conditional Perfect Tense

I would have held
You would have held
One would have held

We would have held
You would have held
They would have held

Conditional Perfect Progressive Tense

I would have been holding
You would have been holding
One would have been holding

We would have been holding
You would have been holding
They would have been holding

Subjunctive Present or Past Tense

I may or might hold
You may or might hold
One may or might hold

We may or might hold
You may or might hold
They may or might hold

Subjunctive Present or Past Perfect Tense

I may[2] or might have held
You may or might have held
One may or might have held

We may or might have held
You may or might have held
They may or might have held

Subjunctive Present or Past Perfect Progressive Tense

I may or might have been holding
You may or might have been holding
One may or might have been holding

We may or might have been holding
You may or might have been holding
They may or might have been holding

Imperative
(You) hold it, or hold on *(informal usage)*.

---

[1] Often contracted: I'd, you'd, we'd, he'd, she'd, they'd.
[2] Subjunctive mood, p.1

Past Participles: laid

Indicative Present Tense

I lay	We lay	**LAY**[1]
You lay	You lay	(transitive)
One[2] lays	They lay	
		LEAD
		(see BLEED)

Past Tense

I laid	We laid	**LEAN**
You laid	You laid	(regular, see
One laid	They laid	SPELL in appendix)

Future Tense

I[3] shall lay	We shall lay	**LEAP**
You will lay	You will lay	(regular,
One will lay	They will lay	see SPELL
		in appendix)

Present or Past Progressive Tense

I[4] am or was laying	We are or were laying	**LEARN**
You are or were laying	You are or were laying	(regular,
One is or was laying	They are or were laying	see SPELL
		in appendix)

Future Progressive Tense

I shall be laying	We shall be laying
You will be laying	You will be laying
One will be laying	They will be laying

Present or Past Perfect Tense

I[5] have or had laid	We have or had laid
You have or had laid	You have or had laid
One has or had laid	They have or had laid

Future Perfect Tense

I[3] shall have laid	We shall have laid
You will have laid	You will have laid
One will have laid	They will have laid

Future Perfect Progressive Tense

I shall have been laying	We shall have been laying
You will have been laying	You will have been laying
One will have been laying	They will have been laying

---

[1] Same conjugations for GAINSAY, MISLAY, OVERLAY, PAY, RELAY (regular, when meaning to relay a message), SAY, WAYLAY.
[2] Also she, he, it.
[3] Often contracted: I'll, you'll, he'll, she'll, we'll, or they'll (shall not: shan't, will not: won't).
[4] Often contracted: I'm, you're, we're, or they're.
[5] Often contracted: I've or I'd, you've or you'd, we've or we'd, or they've or they'd.

Present or Past Perfect Progressive Tense

I have or had been laying
You have or had been laying
One has or had been laying

We have or had been laying
You have or had been laying
They have or had been laying

Conditional (would, should or could)

I[1] would lay
You would lay
One would lay

We would lay
You would lay
They would lay

Conditional Progressive Tense

I would be laying
You would be laying
One would be laying

We would be laying
You would be laying
They would be laying

Conditional Perfect Tense

I would have laid
You would have laid
One would have laid

We would have laid
You would have laid
They would have laid

Conditional Perfect Progressive Tense

I would have been laying
You would have been laying
One would have been laying

We would have been laying
You would have been laying
They would have been laying

Subjunctive Present or Past Tense

I may or might lay
You may or might lay
One may or might lay

We may or might lay
You may or might lay
They may or might lay

Subjunctive Present or Past Perfect Tense

I may[2] or might have laid
You may or might have laid
One may or might have laid

We may or might have laid
You may or might have laid
They may or might have laid

Subjunctive Present or Past Perfect Progressive Tense

I may or might have been laying
You may or might have been laying
One may or might have been laying

We may or might have been laying
You may or might have been laying
They may or might have been laying

Imperative
(You) lay it.

---

[1] Often contracted: I'd, you'd, we'd, he'd, she'd, they'd.
[2] Subjunctive mood, p.1

LEAVE

Past Participle: left

Indicative Present Tense

I leave	We leave
You leave	You leave
One[2] leaves	They leave

Past Tense

I left	We left
You left	You left
One left	They left

Future Tense

I[3] shall leave	We shall leave
You will leave	You will leave
One will leave	They will leave

Present or Past Progressive Tense

I[4] am or was leaving	We are or were leaving
You are or were leaving	You are or were leaving
One is or was leaving	They are or were leaving

Future Progressive Tense

I shall be leaving	We shall be leaving
You will be leaving	You will be leaving
One will be leaving	They will be leaving

Present or Past Perfect Tense

I[5] have or had left	We have or had left
You have or had left	You have or had left
One has or had left	They have or had left

Future Perfect Tense

I[3] shall have left	We shall have left
You will have left	You will have left
One will have left	They will have left

Future Perfect Progressive Tense

I shall have been leaving	We shall have been leaving
You will have been leaving	You will have been leaving
One will have been leaving	They will have been leaving

LEAVE[1]

LEND
(see BEND)

LET
(see invariables)

---

[1] Same conjugations for BEREAVE (also regular), CLEAVE (also regular).
[2] Also she, he, it.
[3] Often contracted: I'll, you'll, he'll, she'll, we'll, or they'll (shall not: shan't, will not: won't).
[4] Often contracted: I'm, you're, we're, or they're.
[5] Often contracted: I've or I'd, you've or you'd, we've or we'd, or they've or they'd.

Present or Past Perfect Progressive Tense

I have or had been leaving
You have or had been leaving
One has or had been leaving

We have or had been leaving
You have or had been leaving
They have or had been leaving

Conditional (would, should or could)

I[1] would leave
You would leave
One would leave

We would leave
You would leave
They would leave

Conditional Progressive Tense

I would be leaving
You would be leaving
One would be leaving

We would be leaving
You would be leaving
They would be leaving

Conditional Perfect Tense

I would have left
You would have left
One would have left

We would have left
You would have left
They would have left

Conditional Perfect Progressive Tense

I would have been leaving
You would have been leaving
One would have been leaving

We would have been leaving
You would have been leaving
They would have been leaving

Subjunctive Present or Past Tense

I may or might leave
You may or might leave
One may or might leave

We may or might leave
You may or might leave
They may or might leave

Subjunctive Present or Past Perfect Tense

I may[2] or might have left
You may or might have left
One may or might have left

We may or might have left
You may or might have left
They may or might have left

Subjunctive Present or Past Perfect Progressive Tense

I may or might have been leaving
You may or might have been leaving
One may or might have been leaving

We may or might have been leaving
You may or might have been leaving
They may or might have been leaving

Imperative

(You) leave (it).

---

[1] Often contracted: I'd, you'd, we'd, he'd, she'd, they'd.
[2] Subjunctive mood, p.1

Past Participles: lain (in a prone position), lied (regular, to tell an untruth)

LIE
(also regular
and intransitive.)

Indicative Present Tense

I lie	We lie
You lie	You lie
One[1] lies	They lie

Past Tense

I lay	We lay
You lay	You lay
One lay	They lay

Future Tense

I[2] shall lie	We shall lie
You will lie	You will lie
One will lie	They will lie

Present or Past Progressive Tense

I[3] am or was lying	We are or were lying
You are or were lying	You are or were lying
One is or was lying	They are or were lying

Future Progressive Tense

I shall be lying	We shall be lying
You will be lying	You will be lying
One will be lying	They will be lying

Present or Past Perfect Tense

I[4] have or had lain	We have or had lain
You have or had lain	You have or had lain
One has or had lain	They have or had lain

Future Perfect Tense

I[2] shall have lain	We shall have lain
You will have lain	You will have lain
One will have lain	They will have lain

Future Perfect Progressive Tense

I shall have been lying	We shall have been lying
You will have been lying	You will have been lying
One will have been lying	They will have been lying

---

[1] Also she, he, it.
[2] Often contracted: I'll, you'll, he'll, she'll, we'll, or they'll (shall not: shan't, will not: won't).
[3] Often contracted: I'm, you're, we're, or they're.
[4] Often contracted: I've or I'd, you've or you'd, we've or we'd, or they've or they'd.

Present or Past Perfect Progressive Tense

I have or had been lying

You have or had been lying

One has or had been lying

We have or had been lying

You have or had been lying

They have or had been lying

Conditional (would, should or could)

I[1] would lie

You would lie

One would lie

We would lie

You would lie

They would lie

Conditional Progressive Tense

I would be lying

You would be lying

One would be lying

We would be lying

You would be lying

They would be lying

Conditional Perfect Tense

I would have lain

You would have lain

One would have lain

We would have lain

You would have lain

They would have lain

Conditional Perfect Progressive Tense

I would have been lying

You would have been lying

One would have been lying

We would have been lying

You would have been lying

They would have been lying

Subjunctive Present or Past Tense

I may or might lie

You may or might lie

One may or might lie

We may or might lie

You may or might lie

They may or might lie

Subjunctive Present or Past Perfect Tense

I may[2] or might have lain

You may or might have lain

One may or might have lain

We may or might have lain

You may or might have lain

They may or might have lain

Subjunctive Present or Past Perfect Progressive Tense

I may or might have been lying

You may or might have been lying

One may or might have been lying

We may or might have been lying

You may or might have been lying

They may or might have been lying

Imperative

(You) lie (there or down).

---

[1] Often contracted: I'd, you'd, we'd, he'd, she'd, they'd.

[2] Subjunctive mood, p.1

Past Participles: lit (transitive: to set fire to), lighted (intransitive: to brighten up or descend)

Indicative Present Tense   **LIGHT[1]**
                                                                                (also regular)

I light	We light
You light	You light
One[2] lights	They light

Past Tense

I lit	We lit
You lit	You lit
One lit	They lit

Future Tense

I[3] shall light	We shall light
You will light	You will light
One will light	They will light

Present or Past Progressive Tense

I[4] am or was lighting	We are or were lighting
You are or were lighting	You are or were lighting
One is or was lighting	They are or were lighting

Future Progressive Tense

I shall be lighting	We shall be lighting
You will be lighting	You will be lighting
One will be lighting	They will be lighting

Present or Past Perfect Tense

I[5] have or had lit	We have or had lit
You have or had lit	You have or had lit
One has or had lit	They have or had lit

Future Perfect Tense

I[3] shall have lit	We shall have lit
You will have lit	You will have lit
One will have lit	They will have lit

Future Perfect Progressive Tense

I shall have been lighting	We shall have been lighting
You will have been lighting	You will have been lighting
One will have been lighting	They will have been lighting

---

[1] Same conjugations for ALIGHT (regular and intransitive when meaning to descend, British use is regular).
[2] Also she, he, it.
[3] Often contracted: I'll, you'll, he'll, she'll, we'll, or they'll (shall not: shan't, will not: won't).
[4] Often contracted: I'm, you're, we're, or they're.
[5] Often contracted: I've or I'd, you've or you'd, we've or we'd, or they've or they'd.

Present or Past Perfect Progressive Tense

I have or had been lighting
You have or had been lighting
One has or had been lighting

We have or had been lighting
You have or had been lighting
They have or had been lighting

Conditional (would, should or could)

I[1] would light
You would light
One would light

We would light
You would light
They would light

Conditional Progressive Tense

I would be lighting
You would be lighting
One would be lighting

We would be lighting
You would be lighting
They would be lighting

Conditional Perfect Tense

I would have lit
You would have lit
One would have lit

We would have lit
You would have lit
They would have lit

Conditional Perfect Progressive Tense

I would have been lighting
You would have been lighting
One would have been lighting

We would have been lighting
You would have been lighting
They would have been lighting

Subjunctive Present or Past Tense

I may or might light
You may or might light
One may or might light

We may or might light
You may or might light
They may or might light

Subjunctive Present or Past Perfect Tense

I may[2] or might have lit
You may or might have lit
One may or might have lit

We may or might have lit
You may or might have lit
They may or might have lit

Subjunctive Present or Past Perfect Progressive Tense

I may or might have been lighting
You may or might have been lighting
One may or might have been lighting

We may or might have been lighting
You may or might have been lighting
They may or might have been lighting

Imperative

(You) light (it.)

---

[1] Often contracted: I'd, you'd, we'd, he'd, she'd, they'd.
[2] Subjunctive mood, p.1

Past Participle: lost

Indicative Present Tense

I lose	We lose
You lose	You lose
One[1] loses	They lose

Past Tense

I lost	We lost
You lost	You lost
One lost	They lost

Future Tense

I[2] shall lose	We shall lose
You will lose	You will lose
One will lose	They will lose

Present or Past Progressive Tense

I[3] am or was losing	We are or were losing
You are or were losing	You are or were losing
One is or was losing	They are or were losing

Future Progressive Tense

I shall be losing	We shall be losing
You will be losing	You will be losing
One will be losing	They will be losing

Present or Past Perfect Tense

I[4] have or had lost	We have or had lost
You have or had lost	You have or had lost
One has or had lost	They have or had lost

Future Perfect Tense

I[2] shall have lost	We shall have lost
You will have lost	You will have lost
One will have lost	They will have lost

Future Perfect Progressive Tense

I shall have been losing	We shall have been losing
You will have been losing	You will have been losing
One will have been losing	They will have been losing

LOSE
(Not to be con-
fused with the
regular verbs:
loose or *loosen*.
See appendix)

---

[1] Also she, he, it.
[2] Often contracted: I'll, you'll, he'll, she'll, we'll, or they'll (shall not: shan't, will not: won't).
[3] Often contracted: I'm, you're, we're, or they're.
[4] Often contracted: I've or I'd, you've or you'd, we've or we'd, or they've or they'd.

Present or Past Perfect Progressive Tense

I have or had been losing
You have or had been losing
One has or had been losing

We have or had been losing
You have or had been losing
They have or had been losing

Conditional (would, should or could)

I[1] would lose
You would lose
One would lose

We would lose
You would lose
They would lose

Conditional Progressive Tense

I would be losing
You would be losing
One would be losing

We would be losing
You would be losing
They would be losing

Conditional Perfect Tense

I would have lost
You would have lost
One would have lost

We would have lost
You would have lost
They would have lost

Conditional Perfect Progressive Tense

I would have been losing
You would have been losing
One would have been losing

We would have been losing
You would have been losing
They would have been losing

Subjunctive Present or Past Tense

I may or might lose
You may or might lose
One may or might lose

We may or might lose
You may or might lose
They may or might lose

Subjunctive Present or Past Perfect Tense

I may[2] or might have lost
You may or might have lost
One may or might have lost

We may or might have lost
You may or might have lost
They may or might have lost

Subjunctive Present or Past Perfect Progressive Tense

I may or might have been losing
You may or might have been losing
One may or might have been losing

We may or might have been losing
You may or might have been losing
They may or might have been losing

Imperative
(You) lose (it).

---

[1] Often contracted: I'd, you'd, we'd, he'd, she'd, they'd.
[2] Subjunctive mood, p.1

MAKE

Past Participle: made

MAKE[1]

Indicative Present Tense

I make	We make
You make	You make
One[2] makes	They make

MAY
(past might,
see auxiliaries)

Past Tense

I made	We made
You made	You made
One made	They made

MEAN
(regular *t*
see appendix)

Future Tense

I[3] shall make	We shall make
You will make	You will make
One will make	They will make

MIGHT
(past of may,
see auxiliaries)

Present or Past Progressive Tense

I[4] am or was making	We are or were making
You are or were making	You are or were making
One is or was making	They are or were making

MISGIVE
(see GIVE)

MISHEAR
(see HEAR)

Future Progressive Tense

I shall be making	We shall be making
You will be making	You will be making
One will be making	They will be making

MISLAY
(see LAY)

MISLEAD
(see BLEED
and invariables)

Present or Past Perfect Tense

I[5] have or had made	We have or had made
You have or had made	You have or had made
One has or had made	They have or had made

MISSPELL
(regular,
see SPELL
in appendix)

Future Perfect Tense

I[3] shall have made	We shall have made
You will have made	You will have made
One will have made	They will have made

MISTAKE
(see TAKE)

Future Perfect Progressive Tense

I shall have been making	We shall have been making
You will have been making	You will have been making
One will have been making	They will have been making

MISUNDERSTAND
(see STAND)

---

[1] Same conjugations for REMAKE, UNMAKE
[2] Also she, he, it.
[3] Often contracted: I'll, you'll, he'll, she'll, we'll, or they'll (shall not: shan't, will not: won't).
[4] Often contracted: I'm, you're, we're, or they're.
[5] Often contracted: I've or I'd, you've or you'd, we've or we'd, or they've or they'd.

Present or Past Perfect Progressive Tense

I have or had been making	We have or had been making
You have been making	You have or had been making
One has or had been making	They have or had been making

Conditional (would, should or could)

I[1] would make	We would make
You would make	You would make
One would make	They would make

Conditional Progressive Tense

I would be making	We would be making
You would be making	You would be making
One would be making	They would be making

Conditional Perfect Tense

I would have made	We would have made
You would have made	You would have made
One would have made	They would have made

Conditional Perfect Progressive Tense

I would have been making	We would have been making
You would have been making	You would have been making
One would have been making	They would have been making

Subjunctive Present or Past Tense

I may or might make	We may or might make
You may or might make	You may or might make
One may or might make	They may or might make

Subjunctive Present or Past Perfect Tense

I may[2] or might have made	We may or might have made
You may or might have made	You may or might have made
One may or might have made	They may or might have made

Subjunctive Present or Past Perfect Progressive Tense

I may or might have been making	We may or might have been making
You may or might have been making	You may or might have been making
One may or might have been making	They may or might have been making

Imperative: (You) make it.

---

[1] Often contracted: I'd, you'd, we'd, he'd, she'd, they'd.
[2] Subjunctive mood, p.1

Past Participles: mown, mowed

Indicative Present Tense

I mow	We mow
You mow	You mow
One[2] mows	They mow

Past Tense

I mowed	We mowed
You mowed	You mowed
One mowed	They mowed

Future Tense

I[3] shall mow	We shall mow
You will mow	You will mow
One will mow	They will mow

Present or Past Progressive Tense

I[4] am or was mowing	We are or were mowing
You are or were mowing	You are or were mowing
One is or was mowing	They are or were mowing

Future Progressive Tense

I shall be mowing	We shall be mowing
You will be mowing	You will be mowing
One will be mowing	They will be mowing

Present or Past Perfect Tense

I[5] have or had mown	We have or had mown
You have or had mown	You have or had mown
One has or had mown	They have or had mown

Future Perfect Tense

I[3] shall have mown	We shall have mown
You will have mown	You will have mown
One will have mown	They will have mown

Future Perfect Progressive Tense

I shall have been mowing	We shall have been mowing
You will have been mowing	You will have been mowing
One will have been mowing	They will have been mowing

---

[1] Same conjugations for ENGRAVE, GRAVE, HEW, LADE, PROVE, RIVE (also regular), ROUGHHEW, SAW, SHAVE, SEW, SHOW (never regular), SOW, STREW, STROW.

[2] Also she, he, it.

[3] Often contracted: I'll, you'll, he'll, she'll, we'll, or they'll (shall not: shan't, will not: won't).

[4] Often contracted: I'm, you're, we're, or they're.

[5] Often contracted: I've or I'd, you've or you'd, we've or we'd, or they've or they'd.

MOW[1]
(also regular)

MUST and OUGHT
(see auxiliaries)

OUTBID
(see invariables)

OUTDO
(see DO)

OUTDRAW
(see BLOW)

OUTGROW
(see BLOW)

OUTRUN
(see RUN)

OUTSELL
(see SELL)

OUTSHINE
(see SHINE)

OUTWEAR
(see WEAR)

OVERBEAR
(see BEAR)

OVERDRAW
(see BLOW)

OVEREAT
(see EAT)

OVERGROW
(See BLOW)

OVERHANG
(see HANG)

OVERHEAR
(see HEAR)

OVERLAY
(see LAY)

OVERLADE
(see MOW)

OVERLIE
(see LIE)

Present or Past Perfect Progressive Tense

I have or had been mowing
You have or had been mowing
One has or had been mowing

We have or had been mowing
You have or had been mowing
They have or had been mowing

Conditional (would, should or could)

I[1] would mow
You would mow
One would mow

We would mow
You would mow
They would mow

Conditional Progressive Tense

I would be mowing
You would be mowing
One would be mowing

We would be mowing
You would be mowing
They would be mowing

Conditional Perfect Tense

I would have mown
You would have mown
One would have mown

We would have mown
You would have mown
They would have mown

Conditional Perfect Progressive Tense

I would have been mowing
You would have been mowing
One would have been mowing

We would have been mowing
You would have been mowing
They would have been mowing

Subjunctive Present or Past Tense

I may or might mow
You may or might mow
One may or might mow

We may or might mow
You may or might mow
They may or might mow

Subjunctive Present or Past Perfect Tense

I may[2] or might have mown
You may or might have mown
One may or might have mown

We may or might have mown
You may or might have mown
They may or might have mown

Subjunctive Present or Past Perfect Progressive Tense

I may or might have been mowing
You may or might have been mowing
One may or might have been mowing

We may or might have been mowing
You may or might have been mowing
They may or might have been mowing

Imperative
(You) mow it.

---

[1] Often contracted: I'd, you'd, we'd, he'd, she'd, they'd.
[2] Subjunctive mood, p.1

OVERPAY
(see LAY)

OVERRIDE
(see RIDE)

OVERRUN
(see RUN)

OVERSEE
(see SEE)

OVERSHOOT
(see SHOOT)

OVERSLEEP
(see SLEEP)

OVERSPEND
(see SPEND)

OVERSPELL
(see SPELL
in appendix)

OVERSPREAD
(see invariables)

OVERSTREW
(see MOW)

OVERSTRIKE
(see STRIKE)

OVERTAKE
(see TAKE)

OVERTHROW
(see BLOW)

OVERTREAD
(See TREAD)

OVERWEAR
(see BEAR)

OVERWRITE
(see WRITE)

PARTAKE
(see TAKE)

PAY
(see LAY)

PEN
(pend *obs.*
see regulars)

PINCH-HIT
(see invariables)

PLEAD
(also regular
see BLEED)

PRESET
(see invariables)

PROVE

Past Participles: proven, proved (Brit.)

Indicative Present Tense

I prove	We prove
You prove	You prove
One[2] proves	They prove

Past Tense

I proved	We proved
You proved	You proved
One proved	They proved

Future Tense

I[3] shall prove	We shall prove
You will prove	You will prove
One will prove	They will prove

Present or Past Progressive Tense

I[4] am or was proving	We are or were proving
You are or were proving	You are or were proving
One is or was proving	They are or were proving

Future Progressive Tense

I shall be proving	We shall be proving
You will be proving	You will be proving
One will be proving	They will be proving

Present or Past Perfect Tense

I[5] have or had proven	We have or had proven
You have or had proven	You have or had proven
One has or had proven	They have or had proven

Future Perfect Tense

I[3] shall have proven	We shall have proven
You will have proven	You will have proven
One will have proven	They will have proven

Future Perfect Progressive Tense

I shall have been proving	We shall have been proving
You will have been proving	You will have been proving
One will have been proving	They will have been proving

---

[1] Same conjugations for *several*, see MOW.
[2] Also she, he, it.
[3] Often contracted: I'll, you'll, he'll, she'll, we'll, or they'll (shall not: shan't, will not: won't).
[4] Often contracted: I'm, you're, we're, or they're.
[5] Often contracted: I've or I'd, you've or you'd, we've or we'd, or they've or they'd.

PROVE[1]
(also regular)

QUICK-FREEZE
(see FREEZE)

REDO
(see DO)

REDRAW
(see BLOW)

REFREEZE
(see FREEZE

REHANG
(see HANG)

REHEAR
(see HEAR)

RELAY
(also regular,
see LAY)

RELIGHT
(see LIGHT)

REMAKE
(see MAKE)

REND
(see BEND)

REPAY
(see LAY)

REREAD
(see invariables)

RERUN
(seeRUN)

RESELL
(see SELL)

RESET
(see invariables)

Present or Past Perfect Progressive Tense

I have or had been proving
You have or had been proving
One has or had been proving

We have or had been proving
You have or had been proving
They have or had been proving

Conditional (would, should or could)

I[1] would prove
You would prove
One would prove

We would prove
You would prove
They would prove

Conditional Progressive Tense

I would be proving
You would be proving
One would be proving

We would be proving
You would be proving
They would be proving

Conditional Perfect Tense

I would have proven
You would have proven
One would have proven

We would have proven
You would have proven
They would have proven

Conditional Perfect Progressive Tense

I would have been proving
You would have been proving
One would have been proving

We would have been proving
You would have been proving
They would have been proving

Subjunctive Present or Past Tense

I may or might prove
You may or might prove
One may or might prove

We may or might prove
You may or might prove
They may or might prove

Subjunctive Present or Past Perfect Tense

I may[2] or might have proven
You may or might have proven
One may or might have proven

We may or might have proven
You may or might have proven
They may or might have proven

Subjunctive Present or Past Perfect Progressive Tense

I may or might have been proving
You may or might have been proving
One may or might have been proving

We may or might have been proving
You may or might have been proving
They may or might have been proving

Imperative
(You) prove (it).

---

[1] Often contracted: I'd, you'd, we'd, he'd, she'd, they'd.
[2] Subjunctive mood, p.1

RESPELL
(see SPELL
in appendix)

RESTRING
(see STRING)

RETAKE
(see TAKE)

RETELL
(see TELL)

RETHINK
(see THINK)

RETREAD
(See TREAD)

REV
(see SPELL
in appendix)

REWIND
(see WIND)

REWRITE
(see WRITE

RID
(also regular, and
invariable. The
regular form, al-
though rare, is
recognized in
American En-
glish. Note the
doubling conso-
nant before the
suffix.)

RIDE

Past Participles: ridden, rode (dial.), rid (rare, dial.)

Indicative Present Tense

I ride	We ride
You ride	You ride
One[2] rides	They ride

Past Tense

I rode	We rode
You rode	You rode
One rode	They rode

Future Tense

I[3] shall ride	We shall ride
You will ride	You will ride
One will ride	They will ride

Present or Past Progressive Tense

I[4] am or was riding	We are or were riding
You are or were riding	You are or were riding
One is or was riding	They are or were riding

Future Progressive Tense

I shall be riding	We shall be riding
You will be riding	You will be riding
One will be riding	They will be riding

Present or Past Perfect Tense

I[5] have or had ridden	We have or had ridden
You have or had ridden	You have or had ridden
One has or had ridden	They have or had ridden

Future Perfect Tense

I[3] shall have ridden	We shall have ridden
You will have ridden	You will have ridden
One will have ridden	They will have ridden

Future Perfect Progressive Tense

I shall have been riding	We shall have been riding
You will have been riding	You will have been riding
One will have been riding	They will have been riding

RIDE[1]

RING
(British term
for calling on
the telephone,
see BEGIN).

---

[1] Same conjugations for BESTRIDE, OVERRIDE, RERIDE, and STRIDE, similar for DRIVE, SMITE, WRITE (these verbs have the same vowel and final consonant changes.)

[2] Also she, he, it.

[3] Often contracted: I'll, you'll, he'll, she'll, we'll, or they'll (shall not: shan't, will not: won't).

[4] Often contracted: I'm, you're, we're, or they're.

[5] Often contracted: I've or I'd, you've or you'd, we've or we'd, or they've or they'd.

Present or Past Perfect Progressive Tense

I have or had been riding
You have or had been riding
One has or had been riding

We have or had been riding
You have or had been riding
They have or had been riding

Conditional (would, should or could)

I[1] would ride
You would ride
One would ride

We would ride
You would ride
They would ride

Conditional Progressive Tense

I would be riding
You would be riding
One would be riding

We would be riding
You would be riding
They would be riding

Conditional Perfect Tense

I would have ridden
You would have ridden
One would have ridden

We would have ridden
You would have ridden
They would have ridden

Conditional Perfect Progressive Tense

I would have been riding
You would have been riding
One would have been riding

We would have been riding
You would have been riding
They would have been riding

Subjunctive Present or Past Tense

I may or might ride
You may or might ride
One may or might ride

We may or might ride
You may or might ride
They may or might ride

Subjunctive Present or Past Perfect Tense

I may[2] or might have ridden
You may or might have ridden
One may or might have ridden

We may or might have ridden
You may or might have ridden
They may or might have ridden

Subjunctive Present or Past Perfect Progressive Tense

I may or might have been riding
You may or might have been riding
One may or might have been riding

We may or might have been riding
You may or might have been riding
They may or might have been riding

Imperative
(You) ride (it).

---

[1] Often contracted: I'd, you'd, we'd, he'd, she'd, they'd.
[2] Subjunctive mood, p.1

Past Participle: risen

Indicative Present Tense

RISE[1]

I rise	We rise
You rise	You rise
One[2] rises	They rise

RIVE
(See Mow)

Past Tense

I rose	We rose
You rose	You rose
One rose	They rose

Future Tense

I[3] shall rise	We shall rise
You will rise	You will rise
One will rise	They will rise

Present or Past Progressive Tense

I[4] am or was rising	We are or were rising
You are or were rising	You are or were rising
One is or was rising	They are or were rising

Future Progressive Tense

I shall be rising	We shall be rising
You will be rising	You will be rising
One will be rising	They will be rising

Present or Past Perfect Tense

I[5] have or had risen	We have or had risen
You have or had risen	You have or had risen
One has or had risen	They have or had risen

Future Perfect Tense

I[3] shall have risen	We shall have risen
You will have risen	You will have risen
One will have risen	They will have risen

Future Perfect Progressive Tense

I shall have been rising	We shall have been rising
You will have been rising	You will have been rising
One will have been rising	They will have been rising

---

[1] Same or similar conjugations for ARISE, RISE, STRIVE, THRIVE (also regular).
[2] Also she, he, it.
[3] Often contracted: I'll, you'll, he'll, she'll, we'll, or they'll (shall not: shan't; will not: won't).
[4] Often contracted: I'm, you're, we're, or they're.
[5] Often contracted: I've or I'd, you've or you'd, we've or we'd, or they've or they'd.

Present or Past Perfect Progressive Tense

I have or had been rising
You have or had been rising
One has or had been rising

We have or had been rising
You have or had been rising
They have or had been rising

Conditional (would, should or could)

I[1] would rise
You would rise
One would rise

We would rise
You would rise
They would rise

Conditional Progressive Tense

I would be rising
You would be rising
One would be rising

We would be rising
You would be rising
They would be rising

Conditional Perfect Tense

I would have risen
You would have risen
One would have risen

We would have risen
You would have risen
They would have risen

Conditional Perfect Progressive Tense

I would have been rising
You would have been rising
One would have been rising

We would have been rising
You would have been rising
They would have been rising

Subjunctive Present or Past Tense

I may or might rise
You may or might rise
One may or might rise

We may or might rise
You may or might rise
They may or might rise

Subjunctive Present or Past Perfect Tense

I may[2] or might have risen
You may or might have risen
One may or might have risen

We may or might have risen
You may or might have risen
They may or might have risen

Subjunctive Present or Past Perfect Progressive Tense

I may or might have been rising
You may or might have been rising
One may or might have been rising

We may or might have been rising
You may or might have been rising
They may or might have been rising

Imperative
(You) rise.

---

[1] Often contracted: I'd, you'd, we'd, he'd, she'd, they'd.
[2] Subjunctive mood, p.1

Past Participle: run

Indicative Present Tense

I run	We run
You run	You run
One[2] runs	They run

Past Tense

I ran	We ran
You ran	You ran
One ran	They ran

Future Tense

I[3] shall run	We shall run
You will run	You will run
One will run	They will run

Present or Past Progressive Tense

I[4] am or was running	We are or were running
You are or were running	You are or were running
One is or was running	They are or were running

Future Progressive Tense

I shall be running	We shall be running
You will be running	You will be running
One will be running	They will be running

Present or Past Perfect Tense

I[5] have or had run	We have or had run
You have or had run	You have or had run
One has or had run	They have or had run

Future Perfect Tense

I[3] shall have run	We shall have run
You will have run	You will have run
One will have run	They will have run

Future Perfect Progressive Tense

I shall have been running	We shall have been running
You will have been running	You will have been running
One will have been running	They will have been running

---

[1] Similar conjugations for COME (same vowel changes, *past* came, *p.p.* come, *progressive* coming.) FORE-RUN, OUTRUN, OVERRUN, RERUN.

[2] Also she, he, it.

[3] Often contracted: I'll, you'll, he'll, she'll, we'll, or they'll (shall not: shan't, will not: won't).

[4] Often contracted: I'm, you're, we're, or they're.

[5] Often contracted: I've or I'd, you've or you'd, we've or we'd, or they've or they'd.

Present or Past Perfect Progressive Tense

I have or had been running	We have or had been running
You have been running	You have or had been running
One has or had been running	They have or had been running

Conditional (would, should or could)

I[1] would run	We would run
You would run	You would run
One would run	They would run

Conditional Progressive Tense

I would be running	We would be running
You would be running	You would be running
One would be running	They would be running

Conditional Perfect Tense

I would have run	We would have run
You would have run	You would have run
One would have run	They would have run

Conditional Perfect Progressive Tense

I would have been running	We would have been running
You would have been running	You would have been running
One would have been running	They would have been running

Subjunctive Present or Past Tense

I may or might run	We may or might run
You may or might run	You may or might run
One may or might run	They may or might run

Subjunctive Present or Past Perfect Tense

I may[2] or might have run	We may or might have run
You may or might have run	You may or might have run
One may or might have run	They may or might have run

Subjunctive Present or Past Perfect Progressive Tense

I may or might have been running	We may or might have been running
You may or might have been running	You may or might have been running
One may or might have been running	They may or might have been running

Imperative: (You) run.

---

[1] Often contracted: I'd, you'd, we'd, he'd, she'd, they'd.
[2] Subjunctive mood, p.1

Past Participles: said

Indicative Present Tense   SAY[1]

I say	We say
You say	You say
One[2] says	They say

Past Tense

I said	We said
You said	You said
One said	They said

Future Tense

I[3] shall say	We shall say
You will say	You will say
One will say	They will say

Present or Past Progressive Tense

I[4] am or was saying	We are or were saying
You are or were saying	You are or were saying
One is or was saying	They are or were saying

Future Progressive Tense

I shall be saying	We shall be saying
You will be saying	You will be saying
One will be saying	They will be saying

Present or Past Perfect Tense

I[5] have or had said	We have or had said
You have or had said	You have or had said
One has or had said	They have or had said

Future Perfect Tense

I[3] shall have said	We shall have said
You will have said	You will have said
One will have said	They will have said

Future Perfect Progressive Tense

I shall have been saying	We shall have been saying
You will have been saying	You will have been saying
One will have been saying	They will have been saying

---

[1] Same conjugations for LAY, PAY
[2] Also she, he, it.
[3] Often contracted: I'll, you'll, he'll, she'll, we'll, or they'll (shall not: shan't, will not: won't).
[4] Often contracted: I'm, you're, we're, or they're.
[5] Often contracted: I've or I'd, you've or you'd, we've or we'd, or they've or they'd.

Present or Past Perfect Progressive Tense

I have or had been saying

You have been saying

One has or had been saying

We have or had been saying

You have or had been saying

They have or had been saying

Conditional (would, should or could)

I[1] would say

You would say

One would say

We would say

You would say

They would say

Conditional Progressive Tense

I would be saying

You would be saying

One would be saying

We would be saying

You would be saying

They would be saying

Conditional Perfect Tense

I would have said

You would have said

One would have said

We would have said

You would have said

They would have said

Conditional Perfect Progressive Tense

I would have been saying

You would have been saying

One would have been saying

We would have been saying

You would have been saying

They would have been saying

Subjunctive Present or Past Tense

I may or might say

You may or might say

One may or might say

We may or might say

You may or might say

They may or might say

Subjunctive Present or Past Perfect Tense

I may[2] or might have said

You may or might have said

One may or might have said

We may or might have said

You may or might have said

They may or might have said

Subjunctive Present or Past Perfect Progressive Tense

I may or might have been saying

You may or might have been saying

One may or might have been saying

We may or might have been saying

You may or might have been saying

They may or might have been saying

Imperative: (You) say it.

---

[1] Often contracted: I'd, you'd, we'd, he'd, she'd, they'd.

[2] Subjunctive mood, p.1

Past Participle: seen

Indicative Present Tense   **SEE[1]**

I see	We see
You see	You see
One[2] sees	They see

SEEK
(see BRING)

Past Tense

I saw	We saw
You saw	You saw
One saw	They saw

Future Tense

I[3] shall see	We shall see
You will see	You will see
One will see	They will see

Present or Past Progressive Tense

I[4] am or was seeing	We are or were seeing
You are or were seeing	You are or were seeing
One is or was seeing	They are or were seeing

Future Progressive Tense

I shall be seeing	We shall be seeing
You will be seeing	You will be seeing
One will be seeing	They will be seeing

Present or Past Perfect Tense

I[5] have or had seen	We have or had seen
You have or had seen	You have or had seen
One has or had seen	They have or had seen

Future Perfect Tense

I[3] shall have seen	We shall have seen
You will have seen	You will have seen
One will have seen	They will have seen

Future Perfect Progressive Tense

I shall have been seeing	We shall have been seeing
You will have been seeing	You will have been seeing
One will have been seeing	They will have been seeing

---

[1] Same conjugations for FORESEE.
[2] Also she, he, it.
[3] Often contracted: I'll, you'll, he'll, she'll, we'll, or they'll (shall not: shan't, will not: won't).
[4] Often contracted: I'm, you're, we're, or they're.
[5] Often contracted: I've or I'd, you've or you'd, we've or we'd, or they've or they'd.

Present or Past Perfect Progressive Tense

I have or had been seeing
You have or had been seeing
One has or had been seeing

We have or had been seeing
You have or had been seeing
They have or had been seeing

Conditional (would, should or could)

I[1] would see
You would see
One would see

We would see
You would see
They would see

Conditional Progressive Tense

I would be seeing
You would be seeing
One would be seeing

We would be seeing
You would be seeing
They would be seeing

Conditional Perfect Tense

I would have seen
You would have seen
One would have seen

We would have seen
You would have seen
They would have seen

Conditional Perfect Progressive Tense

I would have been seeing
You would have been seeing
One would have been seeing

We would have been seeing
You would have been seeing
They would have been seeing

Subjunctive Present or Past Tense

I may or might see
You may or might see
One may or might see

We may or might see
You may or might see
They may or might see

Subjunctive Present or Past Perfect Tense

I may[2] or might have seen
You may or might have seen
One may or might have seen

We may or might have seen
You may or might have seen
They may or might have seen

Subjunctive Present or Past Perfect Progressive Tense

I may or might have been seeing
You may or might have been seeing
One may or might have been seeing

We may or might have been seeing
You may or might have been seeing
They may or might have been seeing

Imperative
(You) see (it.)

---

[1] Often contracted: I'd, you'd, we'd, he'd, she'd, they'd.
[2] Subjunctive mood, p.1

SELL

Past Participle: sold

Indicative Present Tense

I sell	We sell
You sell	You sell
One[2] sells	They sell

Past Tense

I sold	We sold
You sold	You sold
One sold	They sold

Future Tense

I[3] shall sell	We shall sell
You will sell	You will sell
One will sell	They will sell

Present or Past Progressive Tense

I[4] am or was selling	We are or were selling
You are or were selling	You are or were selling
One is or was selling	They are or were selling

Future Progressive Tense

I shall be selling	We shall be selling
You will be selling	You will be selling
One will be selling	They will be selling

Present or Past Perfect Tense

I[5] have or had sold	We have or had sold
You have or had sold	You have or had sold
One has or had sold	They have or had sold

Future Perfect Tense

I[3] shall have sold	We shall have sold
You will have sold	You will have sold
One will have sold	They will have sold

Future Perfect Progressive Tense

I shall have been selling	We shall have been selling
You will have been selling	You will have been selling
One will have been selling	They will have been selling

SELL[1]

SEND
(see BEND)

SET
(see invariables)

SEW
(see MOW)

SHAKE
(see TAKE)

SHALL
(*past* should
see auxiliaries)

---

[1] Same conjugations for OUTSELL, OVERSELL, RESELL, RETELL, TELL, UNDERSELL.
[2] Also she, he, it.
[3] Often contracted: I'll, you'll, he'll, she'll, we'll, or they'll (shall not: shan't, will not: won't).
[4] Often contracted: I'm, you're, we're, or they're.
[5] Often contracted: I've or I'd, you've or you'd, we've or we'd, or they've or they'd.

Present or Past Perfect Progressive Tense

I have or had been selling
You have or had been selling
One has or had been selling

We have or had been selling
You have or had been selling
They have or had been selling

Conditional (would, should or could)

I[1] would sell
You would sell
One would sell

We would sell
You would sell
They would sell

Conditional Progressive Tense

I would be selling
You would be selling
One would be selling

We would be selling
You would be selling
They would be selling

Conditional Perfect Tense

I would have sold
You would have sold
One would have sold

We would have sold
You would have sold
They would have sold

Conditional Perfect Progressive Tense

I would have been selling
You would have been selling
One would have been selling

We would have been selling
You would have been selling
They would have been selling

Subjunctive Present or Past Tense

I may or might sell
You may or might sell
One may or might sell

We may or might sell
You may or might sell
They may or might sell

Subjunctive Present or Past Perfect Tense

I may[2] or might have sold
You may or might have sold
One may or might have sold

We may or might have sold
You may or might have sold
They may or might have sold

Subjunctive Present or Past Perfect Progressive Tense

I may or might have been selling
You may or might have been selling
One may or might have been selling

We may or might have been selling
You may or might have been selling
They may or might have been selling

Imperative
(You) sell it.

---

[1] Often contracted: I'd, you'd, we'd, he'd, she'd, they'd.
[2] Subjunctive mood, p.1

Past Participle: shaven

Indicative Present Tense

I shave	We shave	**SHAVE**[1]
You shave	You shave	(also regular)
One[2] shaves	They shave	

Past Tense

I shaved	We shaved	**SHEAR**
You shaved	You shaved	(see BEAR)
One shaved	They shaved	

Future Tense

I[3] shall shave	We shall shave	**SHED**
You will shave	You will shave	(see invariables)
One will shave	They will shave	

Present or Past Progressive Tense

I[4] am or was shaving	We are or were shaving	**SHEND**
You are or were shaving	You are or were shaving	(see BEND)
One is or was shaving	They are or were shaving	

Future Progressive Tense

I shall be shaving   We shall be shaving
You will be shaving   You will be shaving
One will be shaving   They will be shaving

Present or Past Perfect Tense

I[5] have or had shaved   We have or had shaved
You have or had shaved   You have or had shaved
One has or had shaved   They have or had shaved

Future Perfect Tense

I[3] shall have shaved   We shall have shaved
You will have shaved   You will have shaved
One will have shaved   They will have shaved

Future Perfect Progressive Tense

I shall have been shaving   We shall have been shaving
You will have been shaving   You will have been shaving
One will have been shaving   They will have been shaving

---

[1] Same conjugations for ENGRAVE, GRAVE, HEW, LADE, PROVE, RIVE (British is regular), ROUGH-HEW, SAW, SEW, SHOW (never regular), SOW, STREW, STROW.
[2] Also she, he, it.
[3] Often contracted: I'll, you'll, he'll, she'll, we'll, or they'll (shall not: shan't, will not: won't).
[4] Often contracted: I'm, you're, we're, or they're.
[5] Often contracted: I've or I'd, you've or you'd, we've or we'd, or they've or they'd.

Present or Past Perfect Progressive Tense

I have or had been shaven	We have or had been shaven
You have been shaven	You have or had been shaven
One has or had been shaven	They have or had been shaven

Conditional (would, should or could)

I[1] would shave	We would shave
You would shave	You would shave
One would shave	They would shave

Conditional Progressive Tense

I would be shaving	We would be shaving
You would be shaving	You would be shaving
One would be shaving	They would be shaving

Conditional Perfect Tense

I would have shaven	We would have shaven
You would have shaven	You would have shaven
One would have shaven	They would have shaven

Conditional Perfect Progressive Tense

I would have been shaving	We would have been shaving
You would have been shaving	You would have been shaving
One would have been shaving	They would have been shaving

Subjunctive Present or Past Tense

I may or might	We may or might shaved
You may or might	You may or might shaved
One may or might	They may or might shaved

Subjunctive Present or Past Perfect Tense

I may[2] or might have	We may or might have shaved
You may or might have shaved	You may or might have shaved
One may or might have shaved	They may or might have shaved

Subjunctive Present or Past Perfect Progressive Tense

I may or might have been	We may or might have been shaving
You may or might have been	You may or might have been shaving
One may or might have been shaving	They may or might have been shaving

Imperative: (You) shave (it).

---

[1] Often contracted: I'd, you'd, we'd, he'd, she'd, they'd.
[2] Subjunctive mood, p.1

SHINE

Past Participles: shone (sun), shined (shoes)

Indicative Present Tense

I shine	We shine
You shine	You shine
One[1] shines	They shine

Past Tense

I shone	We shone
You shone	You shone
One shone	They shone

Future Tense

I[2] shall shine	We shall shine
You will shine	You will shine
One will shine	They will shine

Present or Past Progressive Tense

I[3] am or was shining	We are or were shining
You are or were shining	You are or were shining
One is or was shining	They are or were shining

Future Progressive Tense

I shall be shining	We shall be shining
You will be shining	You will be shining
One will be shining	They will be shining

Present or Past Perfect Tense

I[4] have or had shone	We have or had shone
You have or had shone	You have or had shone
One has or had shone	They have or had shone

Future Perfect Tense

I[2] shall have shone	We shall have shone
You will have shone	You will have shone
One will have shone	They will have shone

Future Perfect Progressive Tense

I shall have been shining	We shall have been shining
You will have been shining	You will have been shining
One will have been shining	They will have been shining

SHINE[1]
(also regular)
The irregular past participle refers to the sun or any other shining objects and is intransitive. "The sun shone," or "the brass pot shone brightly." The regular form of the past participle *shined*, is transitive and requires an object to complete the sense of the sentence. "He shined his shoes."

SHOE
(also regular see index)

---

[1] Same conjugations for OUTSHINE, RESHINE.
[2] Also she, he, it.
[3] Often contracted: I'll, you'll, he'll, she'll, we'll, or they'll (shall not: shan't, will not: won't).
[4] Often contracted: I'm, you're, we're, or they're.
[5] Often contracted: I've or I'd, you've or you'd, we've or we'd, or they've or they'd.

Present or Past Perfect Progressive Tense

I have or had been shining
You have or had been shining
One has or had been shining

We have or had been shining
You have or had been shining
They have or had been shining

Conditional (would, should or could)

I[1] would shine
You would shine
One would shine

We would shine
You would shine
They would shine

Conditional Progressive Tense

I would be shining
You would be shining
One would be shining

We would be shining
You would be shining
They would be shining

Conditional Perfect Tense

I would have shone
You would have shone
One would have shone

We would have shone
You would have shone
They would have shone

Conditional Perfect Progressive Tense

I would have been shining
You would have been shining
One would have been shining

We would have been shining
You would have been shining
They would have been shining

Subjunctive Present or Past Tense

I may or might shine
You may or might shine
One may or might shine

We may or might shine
You may or might shine
They may or might shine

Subjunctive Present or Past Perfect Tense

I may[2] or might have shone
You may or might have shone
One may or might have shone

We may or might have shone
You may or might have shone
They may or might have shone

Subjunctive Present or Past Perfect Progressive Tense

I may or might have been shining
You may or might have been shining
One may or might have been shining

We may or might have been shining
You may or might have been shining
They may or might have been shining

Imperative
(You) shine it (up).

---

[1] Often contracted: I'd, you'd, we'd, he'd, she'd, they'd.
[2] Subjunctive mood, p.1

SHOOT

Past Participle: shot

Indicative Present Tense

I shoot	We shoot
You shoot	You shoot
One[1] shoots	They shoot

Past Tense

I shot	We shot
You shot	You shot
One shot	They shot

Future Tense

I[2] shall shoot	We shall shoot
You will shoot	You will shoot
One will shoot	They will shoot

Present or Past Progressive Tense

I[3] am or was shooting	We are or were shooting
You are or were shooting	You are or were shooting
One is or was shooting	They are or were shooting

Future Progressive Tense

I shall be shooting	We shall be shooting
You will be shooting	You will be shooting
One will be shooting	They will be shooting

Present or Past Perfect Tense

I[4] have or had shot	We have or had shot
You have or had shot	You have or had shot
One has or had shot	They have or had shot

Future Perfect Tense

I[2] shall have shot	We shall have shot
You will have shot	You will have shot
One will have shot	They will have shot

Future Perfect Progressive Tense

I shall have been shooting	We shall have been shooting
You will have been shooting	You will have been shooting
One will have been shooting	They will have been shooting

SHOOT[1]

SHOULD
(past of shall see auxiliaries)

SHOW
(see MOW)

SHRED
(see invariables)

SHRINK
(see BEGIN)

SING
(see BEGIN)

SINK
(see BEGIN)

SIT
(see SPIT)

---

[1] Same conjugations for OVERSHOOT, UNDERSHOOT, RESHOOT.
[2] Also she, he, it.
[3] Often contracted: I'll, you'll, he'll, she'll, we'll, or they'll (shall not: shan't, will not: won't).
[4] Often contracted: I'm, you're, we're, or they're.
[5] Often contracted: I've or I'd, you've or you'd, we've or we'd, or they've or they'd.

Present or Past Perfect Progressive Tense

I have or had been shooting
You have or had been shooting
One has or had been shooting

We have or had been shooting
You have or had been shooting
They have or had been shooting

Conditional (would, should or could)

I[1] would shoot
You would shoot
One would shoot

We would shoot
You would shoot
They would shoot

Conditional Progressive Tense

I would be shooting
You would be shooting
One would be shooting

We would be shooting
You would be shooting
They would be shooting

Conditional Perfect Tense

I would have shot
You would have shot
One would have shot

We would have shot
You would have shot
They would have shot

Conditional Perfect Progressive Tense

I would have been shooting
You would have been shooting
One would have been shooting

We would have been shooting
You would have been shooting
They would have been shooting

Subjunctive Present or Past Tense

I may or might shoot
You may or might shoot
One may or might shoot

We may or might shoot
You may or might shoot
They may or might shoot

Subjunctive Present or Past Perfect Tense

I may[2] or might have shot
You may or might have shot
One may or might have shot

We may or might have shot
You may or might have shot
They may or might have shot

Subjunctive Present or Past Perfect Progressive Tense

I may or might have been shooting
You may or might have been shooting
One may or might have been shooting

We may or might have been shooting
You may or might have been shooting
They may or might have been shooting

Imperative
(You) shoot it.

---

[1] Often contracted: I'd, you'd, we'd, he'd, she'd, they'd.
[2] Subjunctive mood, p.1

Past Participle: slain

Indicative Present Tense

I slay	We slay
You slay	You slay
One[1] slays	They slay

Past Tense

I slew	We slew
You slew	You slew
One slew	They slew

Future Tense

I[2] shall slay	We shall slay
You will slay	You will slay
One will slay	They will slay

Present or Past Progressive Tense

I[3] am or was slaying	We are or were slaying
You are or were slaying	You are or were slaying
One is or was slaying	They are or were slaying

Future Progressive Tense

I shall be slaying	We shall be slaying
You will be slaying	You will be slaying
One will be slaying	They will be slaying

Present or Past Perfect Tense

I[4] have or had slain	We have or had slain
You have or had slain	You have or had slain
One has or had slain	They have or had slain

Future Perfect Tense

I[2] shall have slain	We shall have slain
You will have slain	You will have slain
One will have slain	They will have slain

Future Perfect Progressive Tense

I shall have been slaying	We shall have been slaying
You will have been slaying	You will have been slaying
One will have been slaying	They will have been slaying

---

[1] Also she, he, it.
[2] Often contracted: I'll, you'll, he'll, she'll, we'll, or they'll (shall not: shan't, will not: won't).
[3] Often contracted: I'm, you're, we're, or they're.
[4] Often contracted: I've or I'd, you've or you'd, we've or we'd, or they've or they'd.

Present or Past Perfect Progressive Tense

I have or had been slaying	We have or had been slaying
You have or had been slaying	You have or had been slaying
One has or had been slaying	They have or had been slaying

Conditional (would, should or could)

I[1] would slay	We would slay
You would slay	You would slay
One would slay	They would slay

Conditional Progressive Tense

I would be slaying	We would be slaying
You would be slaying	You would be slaying
One would be slaying	They would be slaying

Conditional Perfect Tense

I would have slain	We would have slain
You would have slain	You would have slain
One would have slain	They would have slain

Conditional Perfect Progressive Tense

I would have been slaying	We would have been slaying
You would have been slaying	You would have been slaying
One would have been slaying	They would have been slaying

Subjunctive Present or Past Tense

I may or might slay	We may or might slay
You may or might slay	You may or might slay
One may or might slay	They may or might slay

Subjunctive Present or Past Perfect Tense

I may[2] or might have slain	We may or might have slain
You may or might have slain	You may or might have slain
One may or might have slain	They may or might have slain

Subjunctive Present or Past Perfect Progressive Tense

I may or might have been slaying	We may or might have been slaying
You may or might have been slaying	You may or might have been slaying
One may or might have been slaying	They may or might have been slaying

Imperative
(You) slay it.

---

[1] Often contracted: I'd, you'd, we'd, he'd, she'd, they'd.
[2] Subjunctive mood, p.1

SLEEP

Past Participle: slept

Indicative Present Tense

I sleep	We sleep
You sleep	You sleep
One[2] sleeps	They sleep

Past Tense

I slept	We slept
You slept	You slept
One slept	They slept

Future Tense

I[3] shall sleep	We shall sleep
You will sleep	You will sleep
One will sleep	They will sleep

Present or Past Progressive Tense

I[4] am or was sleeping	We are or were sleeping
You are or were sleeping	You are or were sleeping
One is or was sleeping	They are or were sleeping

Future Progressive Tense

I shall be sleeping	We shall be sleeping
You will be sleeping	You will be sleeping
One will be sleeping	They will be sleeping

Present or Past Perfect Tense

I[5] have or had slept	We have or had slept
You have or had slept	You have or had slept
One has or had slept	They have or had slept

Future Perfect Tense

I[3] shall have slept	We shall have slept
You will have slept	You will have slept
One will have slept	They will have slept

Future Perfect Progressive Tense

I shall have been sleeping	We shall have been sleeping
You will have been sleeping	You will have been sleeping
One will have been sleeping	They will have been sleeping

SLEEP[1]

SLIDE
(Short vowel change for *past* and *p.p.* slid *progressive* sliding, see BLEED.)

SLING
(see SWING)

SLINK
(see SWING)

SMELL
(regular, see SPELL in appendix

SMITE
(see RIDE, also has past participle: *smit*)

SOUND
(linking and regular, see SPELL in appendix.)

SOW
(see MOW)

---

[1] Same conjugations for CREEP, KEEP, LEAP (pronunciation only), OVERSLEEP, UNDERSLEEP, SWEEP, WEEP.

[2] Also she, he, it.

[3] Often contracted: I'll, you'll, he'll, she'll, we'll, or they'll (shall not: shan't, will not: won't).

[4] Often contracted: I'm, you're, we're, or they're.

[5] Often contracted: I've or I'd, you've or you'd, we've or we'd, or they've or they'd.

Present or Past Perfect Progressive Tense

I have or had been sleeping	We have or had been sleeping
You have or had been sleeping	You have or had been sleeping
One has or had been sleeping	They have or had been sleeping

Conditional (would, should or could)

I[1] would sleep	We would sleep
You would sleep	You would sleep
One would sleep	They would sleep

Conditional Progressive Tense

I would be sleeping	We would be sleeping
You would be sleeping	You would be sleeping
One would be sleeping	They would be sleeping

Conditional Perfect Tense

I would have slept	We would have slept
You would have slept	You would have slept
One would have slept	They would have slept

Conditional Perfect Progressive Tense

I would have been sleeping	We would have been sleeping
You would have been sleeping	You would have been sleeping
One would have been sleeping	They would have been sleeping

Subjunctive Present or Past Tense

I may or might sleep	We may or might sleep
You may or might sleep	You may or might sleep
One may or might sleep	They may or might sleep

Subjunctive Present or Past Perfect Tense

I may[2] or might have slept	We may or might have slept
You may or might have slept	You may or might have slept
One may or might have slept	They may or might have slept

Subjunctive Present or Past Perfect Progressive Tense

I may or might have been sleeping	We may or might have been sleeping
You may or might have been sleeping	You may or might have been sleeping
One may or might have been sleeping	They may or might have been sleeping

Imperative
(You) sleep.

---

[1] Often contracted: I'd, you'd, we'd, he'd, she'd, they'd.
[2] Subjunctive mood, p.1

SPEAK

Past Participle: spoken

Indicative Present Tense

I speak	We speak
You speak	You speak
One[2] speaks	They speak

Past Tense

I spoke	We spoke
You spoke	You spoke
One spoke	They spoke

Future Tense

I[3] shall speak	We shall speak
You will speak	You will speak
One will speak	They will speak

Present or Past Progressive Tense

I[4] am or was speaking	We are or were speaking
You are or were speaking	You are or were speaking
One is or was speaking	They are or were speaking

Future Progressive Tense

I shall be speaking	We shall be speaking
You will be speaking	You will be speaking
One will be speaking	They will be speaking

Present or Past Perfect Tense

I[5] have or had spoken	We have or had spoken
You have or had spoken	You have or had spoken
One has or had spoken	They have or had spoken

Future Perfect Tense

I[3] shall have spoken	We shall have spoken
You will have spoken	You will have spoken
One will have spoken	They will have spoken

Future Perfect Progressive Tense

I shall have been speaking	We shall have been speaking
You will have been speaking	You will have been speaking
One will have been speaking	They will have been speaking

SPEAK[1]

SPEED
(see BLEED)

SPELL
(regular, see
appendix)

SPEND
(see BEND)

SPILL
(regular,
see SPELL in
appendix)

---

[1] Same conjugations for BESPEAK, BREAK.
[2] Also she, he, it.
[3] Often contracted: I'll, you'll, he'll, she'll, we'll, or they'll (shall not: shan't, will not: won't).
[4] Often contracted: I'm, you're, we're, or they're.
[5] Often contracted: I've or I'd, you've or you'd, we've or we'd, or they've or they'd.

Present or Past Perfect Progressive Tense

I have or had been speaking
You have or had been speaking
One has or had been speaking

We have or had been speaking
You have or had been speaking
They have or had been speaking

Conditional (would, should or could)

I[1] would speak
You would speak
One would speak

We would speak
You would speak
They would speak

Conditional Progressive Tense

I would be speaking
You would be speaking
One would be speaking

We would be speaking
You would be speaking
They would be speaking

Conditional Perfect Tense

I would have spoken
You would have spoken
One would have spoken

We would have spoken
You would have spoken
They would have spoken

Conditional Perfect Progressive Tense

I would have been speaking
You would have been speaking
One would have been speaking

We would have been speaking
You would have been speaking
They would have been speaking

Subjunctive Present or Past Tense

I may or might speak
You may or might speak
One may or might speak

We may or might speak
You may or might speak
They may or might speak

Subjunctive Present or Past Perfect Tense

I may[2] or might have spoken
You may or might have spoken
One may or might have spoken

We may or might have spoken
You may or might have spoken
They may or might have spoken

Subjunctive Present or Past Perfect Progressive Tense

I may or might have been speaking
You may or might have been speaking
One may or might have been speaking

We may or might have been speaking
You may or might have been speaking
They may or might have been speaking

Imperative

(You) speak (it).

---

[1] Often contracted: I'd, you'd, we'd, he'd, she'd, they'd.
[2] Subjunctive mood, p.1

Past Participles: spun, also span (archaic)

Indicative Present Tense

I spin	We spin
You spin	You spin
One[2] spins	They spin

Past Tense

I spun or span (*British, rare*)	We spun
You spun	You spun
One spun	They spun

Future Tense

I[3] shall spin	We shall spin
You will spin	You will spin
One will spin	They will spin

Present or Past Progressive Tense

I[4] am or was spinning	We are or were spinning
You are or were spinning	You are or were spinning
One is or was spinning	They are or were spinning

Future Progressive Tense

I shall be spinning	We shall be spinning
You will be spinning	You will be spinning
One will be spinning	They will be spinning

Present or Past Perfect Tense

I[5] have or had spun	We have or had spun
You have or had spun	You have or had spun
One has or had spun	They have or had spun

Future Perfect Tense

I[3] shall have spun	We shall have spun
You will have spun	You will have spun
One will have spun	They will have spun

Future Perfect Progressive Tense

I shall have been spinning	We shall have been spinning
You will have been spinning	You will have been spinning
One will have been spinning	They will have been spinning

---

[1] Similar conjugations for FLING (*progressive* flinging), SWING (*progressive* swinging), WRING (*progressive* wringing).

[2] Also she, he, it.

[3] Often contracted: I'll, you'll, he'll, she'll, we'll, or they'll (shall not: shan't, will not: won't).

[4] Often contracted: I'm, you're, we're, or they're.

[5] Often contracted: I've or I'd, you've or you'd, we've or we'd, or they've or they'd.

Present or Past Perfect Progressive Tense

I have or had been spinning
You have been spinning
One has or had been spinning

We have or had been spinning
You have or had been spinning
They have or had been spinning

Conditional (would, should or could)

I[1] would spin
You would spin
One would spin

We would spin
You would spin
They would spin

Conditional Progressive Tense

I would be spinning
You would be spinning
One would be spinning

We would be spinning
You would be spinning
They would be spinning

Conditional Perfect Tense

I would have spun
You would have spun
One would have spun

We would have spun
You would have spun
They would have spun

Conditional Perfect Progressive Tense

I would have been spinning
You would have been spinning
One would have been spinning

We would have been spinning
You would have been spinning
They would have been spinning

Subjunctive Present or Past Tense

I may or might spin
You may or might spin
One may or might spin

We may or might spin
You may or might spin
They may or might spin

Subjunctive Present or Past Perfect Tense

I may[2] or might have spun
You may or might have spun
One may or might have spun

We may or might have spun
You may or might have spun
They may or might have spun

Subjunctive Present or Past Perfect Progressive Tense

I may or might have been spinning
You may or might have been spinning
One may or might have been spinning

We may or might have been spinning
You may or might have been spinning
They may or might have been spinning

Imperative: (You) spin (it).

---

[1] Often contracted: I'd, you'd, we'd, he'd, she'd, they'd.
[2] Subjunctive mood, p.1

SPIT

Past Participles: spat, spit (expectorate), spitted (to cook meat over a fire)

Indicative Present Tense

I spit	We spit
You spit	You spit
One[2] spits	They spit

Past Tense

I spat	We spat
You spat	You spat
One spat	They spat

Future Tense

I[3] shall spit	We shall spit
You will spit	You will spit
One will spit	They will spit

Present or Past Progressive Tense

I[4] am or was spitting	We are or were spitting
You are or were spitting	You are or were spitting
One is or was spitting	They are or were spitting

Future Progressive Tense

I shall be spitting	We shall be spitting
You will be spitting	You will be spitting
One will be spitting	They will be spitting

Present or Past Perfect Tense

I[5] have or had spat	We have or had spat
You have or had spat	You have or had spat
One has or had spat	They have or had spat

Future Perfect Tense

I[3] shall have spat	We shall have spat
You will have spat	You will have spat
One will have spat	They will have spat

Future Perfect Progressive Tense

I shall have been spitting	We shall have been spitting
You will have been spitting	You will have been spitting
One will have been spitting	They will have been spitting

SPIT[1]
(also regular
and invariable,
see appendix)

SPLIT
(see invariables)

SPOIL
(see SPELL
in appendix)

SPREAD
(see invariables)

SPRING
(see BEGIN)

---

[1] Same conjugations for SIT.
[2] Also she, he, it.
[3] Often contracted: I'll, you'll, he'll, she'll, we'll, or they'll (shall not: shan't, will not: won't).
[4] Often contracted: I'm, you're, we're, or they're.
[5] Often contracted: I've or I'd, you've or you'd, we've or we'd, or they've or they'd.

Present or Past Perfect Progressive Tense

I have or had been spitting
You have or had been spitting
One has or had been spitting

We have or had been spitting
You have or had been spitting
They have or had been spitting

Conditional (would, should or could)

I[1] would spit
You would spit
One would spit

We would spit
You would spit
They would spit

Conditional Progressive Tense

I would be spitting
You would be spitting
One would be spitting

We would be spitting
You would be spitting
They would be spitting

Conditional Perfect Tense

I would have spat
You would have spat
One would have spat

We would have spat
You would have spat
They would have spat

Conditional Perfect Progressive Tense

I would have been spitting
You would have been spitting
One would have been spitting

We would have been spitting
You would have been spitting
They would have been spitting

Subjunctive Present or Past Tense

I may or might
spit
You may or might spit
One may or might spit

We may or might spit
You may or might spit
They may or might spit

Subjunctive Present or Past Perfect Tense

I may[2] or might have spat
You may or might have spat
One may or might have spat

We may or might have spat
You may or might have spat
They may or might have spat

Subjunctive Present or Past Perfect Progressive Tense

I may or might have been spitting
You may or might have been spitting
One may or might have been spitting

We may or might have been spitting
You may or might have been spitting
They may or might have been spitting

Imperative

(You) spit (it).

---

[1] Often contracted: I'd, you'd, we'd, he'd, she'd, they'd.
[2] Subjunctive mood, p.1

STAND

Past Participle: stood

Indicative Present Tense

I stand	We stand
You stand	You stand
One[2] stands	They stand

Past Tense

I stood	We stood
You stood	You stood
One stood	They stood

Future Tense

I[3] shall stand	We shall stand
You will stand	You will stand
One will stand	They will stand

Present or Past Progressive Tense

I[4] am or was standing	We are or were standing
You are or were standing	You are or were standing
One is or was standing	They are or were standing

Future Progressive Tense

I shall be standing	We shall be standing
You will be standing	You will be standing
One will be standing	They will be standing

Present or Past Perfect Tense

I[5] have or had stood	We have or had stood
You have or had stood	You have or had stood
One has or had stood	They have or had stood

Future Perfect Tense

I[3] shall have stood	We shall have stood
You will have stood	You will have stood
One will have stood	They will have stood

Future Perfect Progressive Tense

I shall have been standing	We shall have been standing
You will have been standing	You will have been standing
One will have been standing	They will have been standing

STAND[1]

STAVE
(past and *p.p.* stove,
also regular)

---

[1] Same conjugations for MISUNDERSTAND, UNDERSTAND, WITHSTAND.
[2] Also she, he, it.
[3] Often contracted: I'll, you'll, he'll, she'll, we'll, or they'll (shall not: shan't, will not: won't).
[4] Often contracted: I'm, you're, we're, or they're.
[5] Often contracted: I've or I'd, you've or you'd, we've or we'd, or they've or they'd.

Present or Past Perfect Progressive Tense

I have or had been standing
You have or had been standing
One has or had been standing

We have or had been standing
You have or had been standing
They have or had been standing

Conditional (would, should or could)

I[1] would stand
You would stand
One would stand

We would stand
You would stand
They would stand

Conditional Progressive Tense

I would be standing
You would be standing
One would be standing

We would be standing
You would be standing
They would be standing

Conditional Perfect Tense

I would have stood
You would have stood
One would have stood

We would have stood
You would have stood
They would have stood

Conditional Perfect Progressive Tense

I would have been standing
You would have been standing
One would have been standing

We would have been standing
You would have been standing
They would have been standing

Subjunctive Present or Past Tense

I may or might stand
You may or might stand
One may or might stand

We may or might stand
You may or might stand
They may or might stand

Subjunctive Present or Past Perfect Tense

I may[2] or might have stood
You may or might have stood
One may or might have stood

We may or might have stood
You may or might have stood
They may or might have stood

Subjunctive Present or Past Perfect Progressive Tense

I may or might have been standing
You may or might have been standing
One may or might have been standing

We may or might have been standing
You may or might have been standing
They may or might have been standing

Imperative
(You) stand.

---

[1] Often contracted: I'd, you'd, we'd, he'd, she'd, they'd.
[2] Subjunctive mood, p.1

STEAL

Past Participle: stolen

STEAL

STICK
(see SWING)

STING
(see SWING)

STINK
(see SWING)

STREW
(see MOW)

STRIDE
(see RIDE)

Indicative Present Tense

I steal	We steal
You steal	You steal
One[1] steals	They steal

Past Tense

I stole	We stole
You stole	You stole
One stole	They stole

Future Tense

I[2] shall steal	We shall steal
You will steal	You will steal
One will steal	They will steal

Present or Past Progressive Tense

I[3] am or was stealing	We are or were stealing
You are or were stealing	You are or were stealing
One is or was stealing	They are or were stealing

Future Progressive Tense

I shall be stealing	We shall be stealing
You will be stealing	You will be stealing
One will be stealing	They will be stealing

Present or Past Perfect Tense

I[4] have or had stolen	We have or had stolen
You have or had stolen	You have or had stolen
One has or had stolen	They have or had stolen

Future Perfect Tense

I[2] shall have stolen	We shall have stolen
You will have stolen	You will have stolen
One will have stolen	They will have stolen

Future Perfect Progressive Tense

I shall have been stealing	We shall have been stealing
You will have been stealing	You will have been stealing
One will have been stealing	They will have been stealing

---

[1] Also she, he, it.
[2] Often contracted: I'll, you'll, he'll, she'll, we'll, or they'll (shall not: shan't; will not: won't).
[3] Often contracted: I'm, you're, we're, or they're.
[4] Often contracted: I've or I'd, you've or you'd, we've or we'd, or they've or they'd.

Present or Past Perfect Progressive Tense

I have or had been stealing	We have or had been stealing
You have or had been stealing	You have or had been stealing
One has or had been stealing	They have or had been stealing

Conditional (would, should or could)

I[1] would steal	We would steal
You would steal	You would steal
One would steal	They would steal

Conditional Progressive Tense

I would be stealing	We would be stealing
You would be stealing	You would be stealing
One would be stealing	They would be stealing

Conditional Perfect Tense

I would have stolen	We would have stolen
You would have stolen	You would have stolen
One would have stolen	They would have stolen

Conditional Perfect Progressive Tense

I would have been stealing	We would have been stealing
You would have been stealing	You would have been stealing
One would have been stealing	They would have been stealing

Subjunctive Present or Past Tense

I may or might steal	We may or might steal
You may or might steal	You may or might steal
One may or might steal	They may or might steal

Subjunctive Present or Past Perfect Tense

I may[2] or might have stolen	We may or might have stolen
You may or might have stolen	You may or might have stolen
One may or might have stolen	They may or might have stolen

Subjunctive Present or Past Perfect Progressive Tense

I may or might have been stealing	We may or might have been stealing
You may or might have been stealing	You may or might have been stealing
One may or might have been stealing	They may or might have been stealing

Imperative
(You) steal (it).

---

[1] Often contracted: I'd, you'd, we'd, he'd, she'd, they'd.
[2] Subjunctive mood, p.1

Past Participles: struck (to hit or to walk off a job),
stricken (literary, overcome by stress or disease).

Indicative Present Tense　　　　　　　　　　　　　　　　　　　　**STRIKE**[1]

I strike　　　　　　　　　　　　We strike
You strike　　　　　　　　　　　You strike
One[2] strikes　　　　　　　　　They strike

Past Tense

I struck　　　　　　　　　　　　We struck
You struck　　　　　　　　　　　You struck
One struck　　　　　　　　　　　They struck

Future Tense

I[3] shall strike　　　　　　　　We shall strike
You will strike　　　　　　　　You will strike
One will strike　　　　　　　　They will strike

Present or Past Progressive Tense

I[4] am or was striking　　　　We are or were striking
You are or were striking　　　You are or were striking
One is or was striking　　　　They are or were striking

Future Progressive Tense

I shall be striking　　　　　　We shall be striking
You will be striking　　　　　You will be striking
One will be striking　　　　　They will be striking

Present or Past Perfect Tense

I[5] have or had struck　　　　We have or had struck
You have or had struck　　　　You have or had struck
One has or had struck　　　　They have or had struck

Future Perfect Tense

I[3] shall have struck　　　　　We shall have struck
You will have struck　　　　　You will have struck
One will have struck　　　　　They will have struck

Future Perfect Progressive Tense

I shall have been striking　　We shall have been striking
You will have been striking　You will have been striking
One will have been striking　They will have been striking

---

[1] Same or similar conjugations for OVERSTRIKE, RESTRIKE, UNDERSTRIKE.
[2] Also she, he, it.
[3] Often contracted: I'll, you'll, he'll, she'll, we'll, or they'll (shall not: shan't, will not: won't).
[4] Often contracted: I'm, you're, we're, or they're.
[5] Often contracted: I've or I'd, you've or you'd, we've or we'd, or they've or they'd.

Present or Past Perfect Progressive Tense

I have or had been striking	We have or had been striking
You have or had been striking	You have or had been striking
One has or had been striking	They have or had been striking

Conditional (would, should or could)

I[1] would strike	We would strike
You would strike	You would strike
One would strike	They would strike

Conditional Progressive Tense

I would be striking	We would be striking
You would be striking	You would be striking
One would be striking	They would be striking

Conditional Perfect Tense

I would have struck	We would have struck
You would have struck	You would have struck
One would have struck	They would have struck

Conditional Perfect Progressive Tense

I would have been striking	We would have been striking
You would have been striking	You would have been striking
One would have been striking	They would have been striking

Subjunctive Present or Past Tense

I may or might strike	We may or might strike
You may or might strike	You may or might strike
One may or might strike	They may or might strike

Subjunctive Present or Past Perfect Tense

I may[2] or might have struck	We may or might have struck
You may or might have struck	You may or might have struck
One may or might have struck	They may or might have struck

Subjunctive Present or Past Perfect Progressive Tense

I may or might have been striking	We may or might have been striking
You may or might have been striking	You may or might have been striking
One may or might have been striking	They may or might have been striking

Imperative
(You) strike (it).

---

[1] Often contracted: I'd, you'd, we'd, he'd, she'd, they'd.
[2] Subjunctive mood, p.1

STRING

Past Participles: strung (beads), stringed (instruments)

STRING[1]
(also regular)

STRIVE
(see DRIVE)

STROW
(see MOW)

SWAT
(Regular, see
SPELL in appendix.
Same conjugations
for all regular
verbs with short
vowel sounds re-
quiring double
consonants.)

SWEAR
(see BEAR)

Indicative Present Tense

I string	We string
You string	You string
One[2] strings	They string

Past Tense

I strung	We strung
You strung	You strung
One strung	They strung

Future Tense

I[3] shall string	We shall string
You will string	You will string
One will string	They will string

Present or Past Progressive Tense

I[4] am or was stringing	We are or were stringing
You are or were stringing	You are or were stringing
One is or was stringing	They are or were stringing

Future Progressive Tense

I shall be stringing	We shall be stringing
You will be stringing	You will be stringing
One will be stringing	They will be stringing

Present or Past Perfect Tense

I[5] have or had strung	We have or had strung
You have or had strung	You have or had strung
One has or had strung	They have or had strung

Future Perfect Tense

I[3] shall have strung	We shall have strung
You will have strung	You will have strung
One will have strung	They will have strung

Future Perfect Progressive Tense

I shall have been stringing	We shall have been stringing
You will have been stringing	You will have been stringing
One will have been stringing	They will have been stringing

---

[1] Same conjugations for FLING, HANG, WRING; *for others see* SWING.
[2] Also she, he, it.
[3] Often contracted: I'll, you'll, he'll, she'll, we'll, or they'll (shall not: shan't, will not: won't).
[4] Often contracted: I'm, you're, we're, or they're.
[5] Often contracted: I've or I'd, you've or you'd, we've or we'd, or they've or they'd.

Present or Past Perfect Progressive Tense

I have or had been stringing
You have or had been stringing
One has or had been stringing

We have or had been stringing
You have or had been stringing
They have or had been stringing

Conditional (would, should or could)

I[1] would string
You would string
One would string

We would string
You would string
They would string

Conditional Progressive Tense

I would be stringing
You would be stringing
One would be stringing

We would be stringing
You would be stringing
They would be stringing

Conditional Perfect Tense

I would have strung
You would have strung
One would have strung

We would have strung
You would have strung
They would have strung

Conditional Perfect Progressive Tense

I would have been stringing
You would have been stringing
One would have been stringing

We would have been stringing
You would have been stringing
They would have been stringing

Subjunctive Present or Past Tense

I may or might string
You may or might string
One may or might string

We may or might string
You may or might string
They may or might string

Subjunctive Present or Past Perfect Tense

I may[2] or might have strung
You may or might have strung
One may or might have strung

We may or might have strung
You may or might have strung
They may or might have strung

Subjunctive Present or Past Perfect Progressive Tense

I may or might have been stringing
You may or might have been stringing
One may or might have been stringing

We may or might have been stringing
You may or might have been stringing
They may or might have been stringing

Imperative
(You) string it.

---

[1] Often contracted: I'd, you'd, we'd, he'd, she'd, they'd.
[2] Subjunctive mood, p.1

SWELL

Past Participles: swollen, swelled

Indicative Present Tense

I swell	We swell
You swell	You swell
One[1] swells	They swell

Past Tense

I swelled	We swelled
You swelled	You swelled
One swelled	They swelled

Future Tense

I[2] shall swell	We shall swell
You will swell	You will swell
One will swell	They will swell

Present or Past Progressive Tense

I[3] am or was swelling	We are or were swelling
You are or were swelling	You are or were swelling
One is or was swelling	They are or were swelling

Future Progressive Tense

I shall be swelling	We shall be swelling
You will be swelling	You will be swelling
One will be swelling	They will be swelling

Present or Past Perfect Tense

I[4] have or had swollen	We have or had swollen
You have or had swollen	You have or had swollen
One has or had swollen	They have or had swollen

Future Perfect Tense

I[2] shall have swollen	We shall have swollen
You will have swollen	You will have swollen
One will have swollen	They will have swollen

Future Perfect Progressive Tense

I shall have been swelling	We shall have been swelling
You will have been swelling	You will have been swelling
One will have been swelling	They will have been swelling

SWELL
(also regular)

SWEEP
(see SLEEP)

SWIM
(see BEGIN)

---

[1] Also she, he, it.
[2] Often contracted: I'll, you'll, he'll, she'll, we'll, or they'll (shall not: shan't, will not: won't).
[3] Often contracted: I'm, you're, we're, or they're.
[4] Often contracted: I've or I'd, you've or you'd, we've or we'd, or they've or they'd.

Present or Past Perfect Progressive Tense

I have or had been swelling
You have or had been swelling
One has or had been swelling

We have or had been swelling
You have or had been swelling
They have or had been swelling

Conditional (would, should or could)

I[1] would swell
You would swell
One would swell

We would swell
You would swell
They would swell

Conditional Progressive Tense

I would be swelling
You would be swelling
One would be swelling

We would be swelling
You would be swelling
They would be swelling

Conditional Perfect Tense

I would have swollen
You would have swollen
One would have swollen

We would have swollen
You would have swollen
They would have swollen

Conditional Perfect Progressive Tense

I would have been swelling
You would have been swelling
One would have been swelling

We would have been swelling
You would have been swelling
They would have been swelling

Subjunctive Present or Past Tense

I may or might swell
You may or might swell
One may or might swell

We may or might swell
You may or might swell
They may or might swell

Subjunctive Present or Past Perfect Tense

I may[2] or might have swollen
You may or might have swollen
One may or might have swollen

We may or might have swollen
You may or might have swollen
They may or might have swollen

Subjunctive Present or Past Perfect Progressive Tense

I may or might have been swelling
You may or might have been swelling
One may or might have been swelling

We may or might have been swelling
You may or might have been swelling
They may or might have been swelling

Imperative
(You) swell (rarely used).

---

[1] Often contracted: I'd, you'd, we'd, he'd, she'd, they'd.
[2] Subjunctive mood, p.1

SWING

Past Participle: swung

Indicative Present Tense

SWING[1]

I swing	We swing
You swing	You swing
One[2] swings	They swing

Past Tense

I swung	We swung
You swung	You swung
One swung	They swung

Future Tense

I[3] shall swing	We shall swing
You will swing	You will swing
One will swing	They will swing

Present or Past Progressive Tense

I[4] am or was swinging	We are or were swinging
You are or were swinging	You are or were swinging
One is or was swinging	They are or were swinging

Future Progressive Tense

I shall be swinging	We shall be swinging
You will be swinging	You will be swinging
One will be swinging	They will be swinging

Present or Past Perfect Tense

I[5] have or had swung	We have or had swung
You have or had swung	You have or had swung
One has or had swung	They have or had swung

Future Perfect Tense

I[3] shall have swung	We shall have swung
You will have swung	You will have swung
One will have swung	They will have swung

Future Perfect Progressive Tense

I shall have been swinging	We shall have been swinging
You will have been swinging	You will have been swinging
One will have been swinging	They will have been swinging

---

[1] Similar conjugations for CLING, FLING, SLING, SLINK (also regular), SPIN (British past tense also *span,* see BEGIN), STICK, STING, STRING, WRING.

[2] Also she, he, it.

[3] Often contracted: I'll, you'll, he'll, she'll, we'll, or they'll (shall not: shan't, will not: won't).

[4] Often contracted: I'm, you're, we're, or they're.

[5] Often contracted: I've or I'd, you've or you'd, we've or we'd, or they've or they'd.

Present or Past Perfect Progressive Tense

I have or had been swinging
You have or had been swinging
One has or had been swinging

We have or had been swinging
You have or had been swinging
They have or had been swinging

Conditional (would, should or could)

I[1] would swing
You would swing
One would swing

We would swing
You would swing
They would swing

Conditional Progressive Tense

I would be swinging
You would be swinging
One would be swinging

We would be swinging
You would be swinging
They would be swinging

Conditional Perfect Tense

I would have swung
You would have swung
One would have swung

We would have swung
You would have swung
They would have swung

Conditional Perfect Progressive Tense

I would have been swinging
You would have been swinging
One would have been swinging

We would have been swinging
You would have been swinging
They would have been swinging

Subjunctive Present or Past Tense

I may or might swing
You may or might swing
One may or might swing

We may or might swing
You may or might swing
They may or might swing

Subjunctive Present or Past Perfect Tense

I may[2] or might have swung
You may or might have swung
One may or might have swung

We may or might have swung
You may or might have swung
They may or might have swung

Subjunctive Present or Past Perfect Progressive Tense

I may or might have been swinging
You may or might have been swinging
One may or might have been swinging

We may or might have been swinging
You may or might have been swinging
They may or might have been swinging

Imperative

(You) swing (it.)

---

[1] Often contracted: I'd, you'd, we'd, he'd, she'd, they'd.
[2] Subjunctive mood, p.1

TAKE

Past Participle: taken

Indicative Present Tense

I take	We take
You take	You take
One[2] takes	They take

Past Tense

I took	We took
You took	You took
One took	They took

Future Tense

I[3] shall take	We shall take
You will take	You will take
One will take	They will take

Present or Past Progressive Tense

I[4] am or was taking	We are or were taking
You are or were taking	You are or were taking
One is or was taking	They are or were taking

Future Progressive Tense

I shall be taking	We shall be taking
You will be taking	You will be taking
One will be taking	They will be taking

Present or Past Perfect Tense

I[5] have or had taken	We have or had taken
You have or had taken	You have or had taken
One has or had taken	They have or had taken

Future Perfect Tense

I[3] shall have taken	We shall have taken
You will have taken	You will have taken
One will have taken	They will have taken

Future Perfect Progressive Tense

I shall have been taking	We shall have been taking
You will have been taking	You will have been taking
One will have been taking	They will have been taking

TAKE[1]

TASTE
(linking and regular, see appendix.)

---

[1] Same conjugations for BETAKE (archaic), MISTAKE, OVERTAKE, PARTAKE, RETAKE, SHAKE, UNDERTAKE.

[2] Also she, he, it.

[3] Often contracted: I'll, you'll, he'll, she'll, we'll, or they'll (shall not: shan't, will not: won't).

[4] Often contracted: I'm, you're, we're, or they're.

[5] Often contracted: I've or I'd, you've or you'd, we've or we'd, or they've or they'd.

Present or Past Perfect Progressive Tense

I have or had been taking
You have or had been taking
One has or had been taking

We have or had been taking
You have or had been taking
They have or had been taking

Conditional (would, should or could)

I[1] would take
You would take
One would take

We would take
You would take
They would take

Conditional Progressive Tense

I would be taking
You would be taking
One would be taking

We would be taking
You would be taking
They would be taking

Conditional Perfect Tense

I would have taken
You would have taken
One would have taken

We would have taken
You would have taken
They would have taken

Conditional Perfect Progressive Tense

I would have been taking
You would have been taking
One would have been taking

We would have been taking
You would have been taking
They would have been taking

Subjunctive Present or Past Tense

I may or might take
You may or might take
One may or might take

We may or might take
You may or might take
They may or might take

Subjunctive Present or Past Perfect Tense

I may[2] or might have taken
You may or might have taken
One may or might have taken

We may or might have taken
You may or might have taken
They may or might have taken

Subjunctive Present or Past Perfect Progressive Tense

I may or might have been taking
You may or might have been taking
One may or might have been taking

We may or might have been taking
You may or might have been taking
They may or might have been taking

Imperative
(You) take it.

---

[1] Often contracted: I'd, you'd, we'd, he'd, she'd, they'd.
[2] Subjunctive mood, p.1

TEACH

Past Participle: taught

Indicative Present Tense

I teach	We teach
You teach	You teach
One[2] teaches	They teach

Past Tense

I taught	We taught
You taught	You taught
One taught	They taught

Future Tense

I[3] shall teach	We shall teach
You will teach	You will teach
One will teach	They will teach

Present or Past Progressive Tense

I[4] am or was teaching	We are or were teaching
You are or were teaching	You are or were teaching
One is or was teaching	They are or were teaching

Future Progressive Tense

I shall be teaching	We shall be teaching
You will be teaching	You will be teaching
One will be teaching	They will be teaching

Present or Past Perfect Tense

I[5] have or had taught	We have or had taught
You have or had taught	You have or had taught
One has or had taught	They have or had taught

Future Perfect Tense

I[3] shall have taught	We shall have taught
You will have taught	You will have taught
One will have taught	They will have taught

Future Perfect Progressive Tense

I shall have been teaching	We shall have been teaching
You will have been teaching	You will have been teaching
One will have been teaching	They will have been teaching

TEACH[1]

TEAR
(see BEAR)

TELECAST
(see invariables)

TELL
(see SELL)

THINK
(see BRING)

THROW
(see BLOW)

THRUST
(see invariables)

---

[1] Similar conjugations for BESEECH (also regular), BRING, BUY, CATCH, FIGHT, SEEK, THINK, WORK *(past and p.p., respectively, besought, brought, bought, caught, fought, sought, thought, wrought).*
[2] Also she, he, it.
[3] Often contracted: I'll, you'll, he'll, she'll, we'll, or they'll (shall not: shan't, will not: won't).
[4] Often contracted: I'm, you're, we're, or they're.
[5] Often contracted: I've or I'd, you've or you'd, we've or we'd, or they've or they'd.

Present or Past Perfect Progressive Tense

I have or had been teaching	We have or had been teaching
You have been teaching	You have or had been teaching
One has or had been teaching	They have or had been teaching

Conditional (would, should or could)

I[1] would teach	We would teach
You would teach	You would teach
One would teach	They would teach

Conditional Progressive Tense

I would be teaching	We would be teaching
You would be teaching	You would be teaching
One would be teaching	They would be teaching

Conditional Perfect Tense

I would have taught	We would have taught
You would have taught	You would have taught
One would have taught	They would have taught

Conditional Perfect Progressive Tense

I would have been teaching	We would have been teaching
You would have been teaching	You would have been teaching
One would have been teaching	They would have been teaching

Subjunctive Present or Past Tense

I may or might teach	We may or might teach
You may or might teach	You may or might teach
One may or might teach	They may or might teach

Subjunctive Present or Past Perfect Tense

I may[2] or might have taught	We may or might have taught
You may or might have taught	You may or might have taught
One may or might have taught	They may or might have taught

Subjunctive Present or Past Perfect Progressive Tense

I may or might have been teaching	We may or might have been teaching
You may or might have been teaching	You may or might have been teaching
One may or might have been teaching	They may or might have been teaching

Imperative: (You) teach (it).

---

[1] Often contracted: I'd, you'd, we'd, he'd, she'd, they'd.
[2] Subjunctive mood, p.1

TREAD

Past Participles: trodden, trod, treaded (American English)

Indicative Present Tense

I tread	We tread
You tread	You tread
One[1] treads	They tread

Past Tense

I trod (or treaded)	We trod
You trod	You trod
One trod	They trod

Future Tense

I[2] shall tread	We shall tread
You will tread	You will tread
One will tread	They will tread

Present or Past Progressive Tense

I[3] am or was treading	We are or were treading
You are or were treading	You are or were treading
One is or was treading	They are or were treading

Future Progressive Tense

I shall be treading	We shall be treading
You will be treading	You will be treading
One will be treading	They will be treading

Present or Past Perfect Tense

I[4] have or had trodden	We have or had trodden
You have or had trodden	You have or had trodden
One has or had trodden	They have or had trodden

Future Perfect Tense

I[2] shall have trodden	We shall have trodden
You will have trodden	You will have trodden
One will have trodden	They will have trodden

Future Perfect Progressive Tense

I shall have been treading	We shall have been treading
You will have been treading	You will have been treading
One will have been treading	They will have been treading

TREAD
(transitive and intransitive, also regular in American English.)

UNBEND
(see BEND)

UNBIND
(see BIND)

UNDERGO
(see GO)

UNDERLAY
(see LAY)

UNDERLIE
(see LIE)

UNDERPAY
(see LAY)

UNDERSELL
(see SELL)

UNDERSHOOT
(see SHOOT)

UNDERSTAND
(see STAND)

UNDERTAKE
(see TAKE)

UNDERTREAD
(See TREAD)

UNDERWRITE
(see WRITE)

---

[1] Same conjugations as OVERTREAD, RETREAD and UNDERTREAD.
[2] Also she, he, it.
[3] Often contracted: I'll, you'll, he'll, she'll, we'll, or they'll (shall not: shan't, will not: won't).
[4] Often contracted: I'm, you're, we're, or they're.
[5] Often contracted: I've or I'd, you've or you'd, we've or we'd, or they've or they'd.

Present or Past Perfect Progressive Tense

I have or had been treading	We have or had been treading
You have or had been treading	You have or had been treading
One has or had been treading	They have or had been treading

Conditional (would, should or could)

I[1] would tread	We would tread
You would tread	You would tread
One would tread	They would tread

Conditional Progressive Tense

I would be treading	We would be treading
You would be treading	You would be treading
One would be treading	They would be treading

Conditional Perfect Tense

I would have trodden	We would have trodden
You would have trodden	You would have trodden
One would have trodden	They would have trodden

Conditional Perfect Progressive Tense

I would have been treading	We would have been treading
You would have been treading	You would have been treading
One would have been treading	They would have been treading

Subjunctive Present or Past Tense

I may or might tread	We may or might tread
You may or might tread	You may or might tread
One may or might tread	They may or might tread

Subjunctive Present or Past Perfect Tense

I may[2] or might have trodden	We may or might have trodden
You may or might have trodden	You may or might have trodden
One may or might have trodden	They may or might have trodden

Subjunctive Present or Past Perfect Progressive Tense

I may or might have been treading	We may or might have been treading
You may or might have been treading	You may or might have been treading
One may or might have been treading	They may or might have been treading

Imperative
(You) tread (it).

---

[1] Often contracted: I'd, you'd, we'd, he'd, she'd, they'd.
[2] Subjunctive mood, p.1

UNDO
(see DO)

UNWIND
(see BIND)

UPHOLD
(see HOLD)

WAKE
(see AWAKE)

WAYLAY
(see LAY)

WEAR
(see BEAR)

WEAVE
(see HEAVE)

WEEP
(see SLEEP)

WET
(see invariables)

WILL
(past would
also regular,
see auxiliaries.)

Past Participle: won

Indicative Present Tense

I win	We win
You win	You win
One[1] wins	They win

Past Tense

I won	We won
You won	You won
One won	They won

Future Tense

I[2] shall win	We shall win
You will win	You will win
One will win	They will win

Present or Past Progressive Tense

I[3] am or was winning	We are or were winning
You are or were winning	You are or were winning
One is or was winning	They are or were winning

Future Progressive Tense

I shall be winning	We shall be winning
You will be winning	You will be winning
One will be winning	They will be winning

Present or Past Perfect Tense

I[4] have or had won	We have or had won
You have or had won	You have or had won
One has or had won	They have or had won

Future Perfect Tense

I[2] shall have won	We shall have won
You will have won	You will have won
One will have won	They will have won

Future Perfect Progressive Tense

I shall have been winning	We shall have been winning
You will have been winning	You will have been winning
One will have been winning	They will have been winning

WIN

WIND
(see BIND)

WITHDRAW
(see DRAW)

WITHHOLD
(see HOLD)

WITHSTAND
(see STAND)

---

[1] Also she, he, it.
[2] Often contracted: I'll, you'll, he'll, she'll, we'll, or they'll (shall not: shan't, will not: won't).
[3] Often contracted: I'm, you're, we're, or they're.
[4] Often contracted: I've or I'd, you've or you'd, we've or we'd, or they've or they'd.

Present or Past Perfect Progressive Tense

I have or had been winning	We have or had been winning
You have or had been winning	You have or had been winning
One has or had been winning	They have or had been winning

Conditional (would, should or could)

I[1] would win	We would win
You would win	You would win
One would win	They would win

Conditional Progressive Tense

I would be winning	We would be winning
You would be winning	You would be winning
One would be winning	They would be winning

Conditional Perfect Tense

I would have won	We would have won
You would have won	You would have won
One would have won	They would have won

Conditional Perfect Progressive Tense

I would have been winning	We would have been winning
You would have been winning	You would have been winning
One would have been winning	They would have been winning

Subjunctive Present or Past Tense

I may or might win	We may or might win
You may or might win	You may or might win
One may or might win	They may or might win

Subjunctive Present or Past Perfect Tense

I may[2] or might have won	We may or might have won
You may or might have won	You may or might have won
One may or might have won	They may or might have won

Subjunctive Present or Past Perfect Progressive Tense

I may or might have been winning	We may or might have been winning
You may or might have been winning	You may or might have been winning
One may or might have been winning	They may or might have been winning

Imperative
(You) win.

---

[1] Often contracted: I'd, you'd, we'd, he'd, she'd, they'd.
[2] Subjunctive mood, p.1

WORK

Past Participles: wrought (to forge a shape), worked (employment)

Indicative Present Tense

I work	We work
You work	You work
One[1] works	They work

Past Tense

I wrought	We wrought
You wrought	You wrought
One wrought	They wrought

Future Tense

I[2] shall work	We shall work
You will work	You will work
One will work	They will work

Present or Past Progressive Tense

I[3] am or was working	We are or were working
You are or were working	You are or were working
One is or was working	They are or were working

Future Progressive Tense

I shall be working	We shall be working
You will be working	You will be working
One will be working	They will be working

Present or Past Perfect Tense

I[4] have or had wrought	We have or had wrought
You have or had wrought	You have or had wrought
One has or had wrought	They have or had wrought

Future Perfect Tense

I[2] shall have wrought	We shall have wrought
You will have wrought	You will have wrought
One will have wrought	They will have wrought

Future Perfect Progressive Tense

I shall have been working	We shall have been working
You will have been working	You will have been working
One will have been working	They will have been working

WORK[1]
(also regular)

WOULD
(see auxiliaries
past of will)

WRING
(see STRING)

---

[1] Similar conjugations for BESEECH, BRING, BUY, CATCH, FIGHT, SEEK, TEACH, THINK, *(past and p.p., respectively, besought, brought, bought, caught, fought, sought, taught, thought).*

[2] Also she, he, it.

[3] Often contracted: I'll, you'll, he'll, she'll, we'll, or they'll (shall not: shan't, will not: won't).

[4] Often contracted: I'm, you're, we're, or they're.

[5] Often contracted: I've or I'd, you've or you'd, we've or we'd, or they've or they'd.

Present or Past Perfect Progressive Tense

I have or had been working
You have or had been working
One has or had been working

We have or had been working
You have or had been working
They have or had been working

Conditional (would, should or could)

I[1] would work
You would work
One would work

We would work
You would work
They would work

Conditional Progressive Tense

I would be working
You would be working
One would be working

We would be working
You would be working
They would be working

Conditional Perfect Tense

I would have wrought
You would have wrought
One would have wrought

We would have wrought
You would have wrought
They would have wrought

Conditional Perfect Progressive Tense

I would have been working
You would have been working
One would have been working

We would have been working
You would have been working
They would have been working

Subjunctive Present or Past Tense

I may or might work
You may or might work
One may or might work

We may or might work
You may or might work
They may or might work

Subjunctive Present or Past Perfect Tense

I may[2] or might have wrought
You may or might have wrought
One may or might have wrought

We may or might have wrought
You may or might have wrought
They may or might have wrought

Subjunctive Present or Past Perfect Progressive Tense

I may or might have been working
You may or might have been working
One may or might have been working

We may or might have been working
You may or might have been working
They may or might have been working

Imperative
(You) work (it).

---

[1] Often contracted: I'd, you'd, we'd, he'd, she'd, they'd.
[2] Subjunctive mood, p.1

Past Participle: written

Indicative Present Tense

WRITE[1]

I write
You write
One[2] writes

We write
You write
They write

Past Tense

I wrote
You wrote
One wrote

We wrote
You wrote
They wrote

Future Tense

I[3] shall write
You will write
One will write

We shall write
You will write
They will write

Present or Past Progressive Tense

I[4] am or was writing
You are or were writing
One is or was writing

We are or were writing
You are or were writing
They are or were writing

Future Progressive Tense

I shall be writing
You will be writing
One will be writing

We shall be writing
You will be writing
They will be writing

Present or Past Perfect Tense

I[5] have or had written
You have or had written
One has or had written

We have or had written
You have or had written
They have or had written

Future Perfect Tense

I[3] shall have written
You will have written
One will have written

We shall have written
You will have written
They will have written

Future Perfect Progressive Tense

I shall have been writing
You will have been writing
One will have been writing

We shall have been writing
You will have been writing
They will have been writing

---

[1] Similar conjugations for OVERRIDE, OVERWRITE, REWRITE, RIDE, SMITE, STRIDE, UNDER-WRITE. (Same vowel changes occur in: OVERRIDE, RIDE, *past* rode, *p.p.* ridden, and STRIDE.)
[2] Also she, he, it.
[3] Often contracted: I'll, you'll, he'll, she'll, we'll, or they'll (shall not: shan't, will not: won't).
[4] Often contracted: I'm, you're, we're, or they're.
[5] Often contracted: I've or I'd, you've or you'd, we've or we'd, or they've or they'd.

Present or Past Perfect Progressive Tense

I have or had been writing
You have or had been writing
One has or had been writing

We have or had been writing
You have or had been writing
They have or had been writing

Conditional (would, should or could)

I[1] would write
You would write
One would write

We would write
You would write
They would write

Conditional Progressive Tense

I would be writing
You would be writing
One would be writing

We would be writing
You would be writing
They would be writing

Conditional Perfect Tense

I would have written
You would have written
One would have written

We would have written
You would have written
They would have written

Conditional Perfect Progressive Tense

I would have been writing
You would have been writing
One would have been writing

We would have been writing
You would have been writing
They would have been writing

Subjunctive Present or Past Tense

I may or might write
You may or might write
One may or might write

We may or might write
You may or might write
They may or might write

Subjunctive Present or Past Perfect Tense

I may[2] or might have written
You may or might have written
One may or might have written

We may or might have written
You may or might have written
They may or might have written

Subjunctive Present or Past Perfect Progressive Tense

I may or might have been writing
You may or might have been writing
One may or might have been writing

We may or might have been writing
You may or might have been writing
They may or might have been writing

Imperative
(You) write it.

---

[1] Often contracted: I'd, you'd, we'd, he'd, she'd, they'd.
[2] Subjunctive mood, p.1

APPENDIX

An Example of a Regular Verb: SPELL

Past Participles: spelled, spelt (British)

Indicative Present Tense

I spell	We spell
You spell	You spell
One[1] spells	They spell

Past Tense

I spelled	We spelled
You spelled	You spelled
One spelled	They spelled

Future Tense

I[2] shall spell	We shall spell
You will spell	You will spell
One will spell	They will spell

Present or Past Progressive Tense

I[3] am or was spelling	We are or were spelling
You are or were spelling	You are or were spelling
One is or was spelling	They are or were spelling

Future Progressive Tense

I shall be spelling	We shall be spelling
You will be spelling	You will be spelling
One will be spelling	They will be spelling

Present or Past Perfect Tense

I[4] have or had spelled	We have or had spelled
You have or had spelled	You have or had spelled
One has or had spelled	They have or had spelled

Future Perfect Tense

I[2] shall have spelled	We shall have spelled
You will have spelled	You will have spelled
One will have spelled	They will have spelled

Future Perfect Progressive Tense

I shall have been spelling	We shall have been spelling
You will have been spelling	You will have been spelling
One will have been spelling	They will have been spelling

SPELL

Other *t* or *ed* endings:

BURN
DREAM
GELD
GILD
GIRD
LEAN
LEARN
LEAP
PEN
REND
SEND
SPOIL

Change *l* for *t* or *ed*:

DWELL
SMELL
SPELL
SPILL

Only *t* endings:

BUILD
DEAL
MEAN
MISDEAL

Only *d* endings:
(in regular form)

ABIDE
BEREAVE
CHIDE
CLEAVE
CLOTHE
DARE
DIVE
HEAVE
LADE
LIE
LOOSE
SHINE
SHOE
STAVE
STRIVE
TASTE

---

[1] Also she, he, it.
[2] Often contracted: I'll, you'll, he'll, she'll, we'll, or they'll (shall not: shan't, will not: won't).
[3] Often contracted: I'm, you're, we're, or they're.
[4] Often contracted: I've or I'd, you've or you'd, we've or we'd, or they've or they'd.

SPELL

Present or Past Perfect Progressive Tense

I have or had been spelling
You have or had been spelling
One has or had been spelling

We have or had been spelling
You have or had been spelling
They have or had been spelling

Conditional (would, should or could)

I[1] would spell
You would spell
One would spell

We would spell
You would spell
They would spell

Conditional Progressive Tense

I would be spelling
You would be spelling
One would be spelling

We would be spelling
You would be spelling
They would be spelling

Conditional Perfect Tense

I would have spelled
You would have spelled
One would have spelled

We would have spelled
You would have spelled
They would have spelled

Conditional Perfect Progressive Tense

I would have been spelling
You would have been spelling
One would have been spelling

We would have been spelling
You would have been spelling
They would have been spelling

Subjunctive Present or Past Tense

I may or might spell
You may or might spell
One may or might spell

We may or might spell
You may or might spell
They may or might spell

Subjunctive Present or Past Perfect Tense

I may[2] or might have spelled
You may or might have spelled
One may or might have spelled

We may or might have spelled
You may or might have spelled
They may or might have spelled

Subjunctive Present or Past Perfect Progressive Tense

I may or might have been spelling
You may or might have been spelling
One may or might have been spelling

We may or might have been spelling
You may or might have been spelling
They may or might have been spelling

Imperative
(You) spell (it).

---

[1] Often contracted: I'd, you'd, we'd, he'd, she'd, they'd.
[2] Subjunctive mood, p.1

Only *ed* endings:
(in regular form)

APPEAR
BELAY
BESEECH
BESTEAD
BLEND
DREAM
HEW
LIGHT
LOOSEN
PLEAD
RELAY
REMAIN
RETREAD
SEEM
SOUND
STREW
STRING
STROW
SWELL
TREAD
TURN
WILL
WORK

Doubling Consonants and *ed*:

BIT
DWELL
PEN
REV
RID
SPIT
SWAT
TREK
WED

Change *d* to *t* endings:

SPEND
(see BEND)

An Example of a Regular "Y" Ending Verb: CRY

Past Participle: cried

Indicative Present Tense

		CRY
I cry	We cry	
You cry	You cry	Common form
One[1] cries	They cry	for all verbs end-

Past Tense

ing in "y."
Change "y" to *i*

		and add *es* or *ed*,
I cried	We cried	but keep "y"
You cried	You cried	when adding
One cried	They cried	"ing."

Future Tense

Exceptions: "y" is

		retained in end
I[2] shall cry	We shall cry	sounding suffixes
You will cry	You will cry	like *ee*, as in *vol-*
One will cry	They will cry	*ley*, or *a*, as in *be-*

Present or Past Progressive Tense

tray, *fray*, *play*,

		pray, and *stray*.
I[3] am or was crying	We are or were crying	
You are or were crying	You are or were crying	
One is or was crying	They are or were crying	

Future Progressive Tense

I shall be crying	We shall be crying
You will be crying	You will be crying
One will be crying	They will be crying

Present or Past Perfect Tense

I[4] have or had cried	We have or had cried
You have or had cried	You have or had cried
One has or had cried	They have or had cried

Future Perfect Tense

I[2] shall have cried	We shall have cried
You will have cried	You will have cried
One will have cried	They will have cried

Future Perfect Progressive Tense

I shall have been crying	We shall have been crying
You will have been crying	You will have been crying
One will have been crying	They will have been crying

---

[1] Also she, he, it.
[2] Often contracted: I'll, you'll, he'll, she'll, we'll, or they'll (shall not: shan't, will not: won't).
[3] Often contracted: I'm, you're, we're, or they're.
[4] Often contracted: I've or I'd, you've or you'd, we've or we'd, or they've or they'd.

CRY

Present or Past Perfect Progressive Tense

I have or had been crying
You have or had been crying
One has or had been crying

We have or had been crying
You have or had been crying
They have or had been crying

Conditional (would, should or could)

I[1] would cry
You would cry
One would cry

We would cry
You would cry
They would cry

Conditional Progressive Tense

I would be crying
You would be crying
One would be crying

We would be crying
You would be crying
They would be crying

Conditional Perfect Tense

I would have cried
You would have cried
One would have cried

We would have cried
You would have cried
They would have cried

Conditional Perfect Progressive Tense

I would have been crying
You would have been crying
One would have been crying

We would have been crying
You would have been crying
They would have been crying

Subjunctive Present or Past Tense

I may or might cry
You may or might cry
One may or might cry

We may or might cry
You may or might cry
They may or might cry

Subjunctive Present or Past Perfect Tense

I may[2] or might have cried
You may or might have cried
One may or might have cried

We may or might have cried
You may or might have cried
They may or might have cried

Subjunctive Present or Past Perfect Progressive Tense

I may or might have been crying
You may or might have been crying
One may or might have been crying

We may or might have been crying
You may or might have been crying
They may or might have been crying

Imperative

(You) cry.

---

[1] Often contracted: I'd, you'd, we'd, he'd, she'd, they'd.
[2] Subjunctive mood, p.1

An Example of Invariable or Set Verbs: PUT

Past Participle: put

		PUT[1]
Indicative Present Tense		

Indicative Present Tense

I put	We put	Common form for all
You put	You put	set verbs as in:
One[2] puts	They put	

Past Tense

		BET
		(rarely regular)
I put	We put	BID
You put	You put	BURST
One put	They put	CAST
		COST

Future Tense

		CUT
		FIT
I[3] shall put	We shall put	FORECAST
You will put	You will put	HIT
One will put	They will put	HURT

Present or Past Progressive Tense

		KNIT
I[4] am or was putting	We are or were putting	(also regular knitted)
You are or were putting	You are or were putting	LET
One is or was putting	They are or were putting	MISCAST
		MISREAD

Future Progressive Tense

		OUTBID
I shall be putting	We shall be putting	OVERSPREAD
You will be putting	You will be putting	PINCH-HIT
One will be putting	They will be putting	PRESET
		PUT

Present or Past Perfect Tense

		QUIT
I[5] have or had put	We have or had put	READ
You have or had put	You have or had put	(*past* and *p.p.*
One has or had put	They have or had put	pronounced *red.*)
		REREAD

Future Perfect Tense

		(*past* and *p.p.*
I[3] shall have put	We shall have put	pronounced *red.*)
You will have put	You will have put	RESET
One will have put	They will have put	RID

Future Perfect Progressive Tense

		(rarely regular)
I shall have been putting	We shall have been putting	SET
You will have been putting	You will have been putting	
One will have been putting	They will have been putting	

---

[1] Same conjugations for all set verbs
[2] Also she, he, it.
[3] Often contracted: I'll, you'll, he'll, she'll, we'll, or they'll (shall not: shan't, will not: won't).
[4] Often contracted: I'm, you're, we're, or they're.
[5] Often contracted: I've or I'd, you've or you'd, we've or we'd, or they've or they'd.

PUT

Present or Past Perfect Progressive Tense

I have or had been putting
You have been putting
One has or had been putting

We have or had been putting
You have or had been putting
They have or had been putting

Conditional (would, should or could)

I[1] would put
You would put
One would put

We would put
You would put
They would put

Conditional Progressive Tense

I would be putting
You would be putting
One would be putting

We would be putting
You would be putting
They would be putting

Conditional Perfect Tense

I would have put
You would have put
One would have put

We would have put
You would have put
They would have put

Conditional Perfect Progressive Tense

I would have been putting
You would have been putting
One would have been putting

We would have been putting
You would have been putting
They would have been putting

Subjunctive Present or Past Tense

I may or might put
You may or might put
One may or might put

We may or might put
You may or might put
They may or might put

Subjunctive Present or Past Perfect Tense

I may[2] or might have put
You may or might have put
One may or might have put

We may or might have put
You may or might have put
They may or might have put

Subjunctive Present or Past Perfect Progressive Tense

I may or might have been putting
You may or might have been putting
One may or might have been putting

We may or might have been putting
You may or might have been putting
They may or might have been putting

Imperative
(You) put it there, on or down.

SHED
SHRED
SHUT
SIMULCAST
SLIT
SPIT
SPLIT
SPREAD
TELECAST
THRUST
TYPECAST
UNDERBID
UNDERCUT
UPSET
WED
(also regular
wedded)
WET

---

[1] Often contracted: I'd, you'd, we'd, he'd, she'd, they'd.
[2] Subjunctive mood, p.1

An Example of a Passive Voice Verb: BE GROWN

Past Participle: grown

Indicative Present Tense

I am grown
You are grown
One[2] is grown

We are grown
You are grown
They are grown

Past Tense

I was grown
You were grown
One was grown

We were grown
You were grown
They were grown

Future Tense

I[3] shall be grown
You will be grown
One will be grown

We shall be grown
You will be grown
They will be grown

Present or Past Progressive Tense

I[4] am or was being grown
You are or were being grown
One is or was being grown

We are or were being grown
You are or were being grown
They are or were being grown

Future Progressive Tense

I shall be being grown
You will be being grown
One will be being grown

We shall be being grown
You will be being grown
They will be being grown

Present or Past Perfect Tense

I[5] have or had been grown
You have or had been grown
One has or had been grown

We have or had been grown
You have or had been grown
They have or had been grown

Future Perfect Tense

I[3] shall have been grown
You will have been grown
One will have been grown

We shall have been grown
You will have been grown
They will have been grown

Future Perfect Progressive Tense

I shall have been being grown
You will have been being grown
One will have been being grown

We shall have been being grown
You will have been being grown
They will have been being grown

BE GROWN[1]
Same form for all verbs in passive voice: conjugate *be* and use the past participle of the verb.

BE FROSTBITTEN
Most verbs may be cast in the passive voice, but there are some that can never be active. This is because there is no subject to perform their action. In the case of *frostbite,* this verb is always passive because its obvious subject, the weather or ice, is inanimate and cannot possibly produce a conscious act.

---

[1] Same conjugations for all passive voice forms
[2] Also she, he, it.
[3] Often contracted: I'll, you'll, he'll, she'll, we'll, or they'll (shall not: shan't, will not: won't).
[4] Often contracted: I'm, you're, we're, or they're.
[5] Often contracted: I've or I'd, you've or you'd, we've or we'd, or they've or they'd.

BE GROWN

Present or Past Perfect Progressive Tense

I have or had been being grown
You have been being grown
One has or had been being grown

We have or had been being grown
You have or had been being grown
They have or had been being grown

Conditional (would, should or could)

I[1] would be grown
You would be grown
One would be grown

We would be grown
You would be grown
They would be grown

Conditional Progressive Tense

I would be being grown
You would be being grown
One would be being grown

We would be being grown
You would be being grown
They would be being grown

Conditional Perfect Tense

I would have been grown
You would have been grown
One would have been grown

We would have been grown
You would have been grown
They would have been grown

Conditional Perfect Progressive Tense

I would have been being grown
You would have been being grown
One would have been being grown

We would have been being grown
You would have been being grown
They would have been being grown

Subjunctive Present or Past Tense

I may or might be grown
You may or might be grown
One may or might be grown

We may or might be grown
You may or might be grown
They may or might be grown

Subjunctive Present or Past Perfect Tense

I may[2] or might have been grown
You may or might have been grown
One may or might have been grown

We may or might have been grown
You may or might have been grown
They may or might have been grown

Subjunctive Present or Past Perfect Progressive Tense

I may or might have been being grown
You may or might have been being grown
One may or might have been being grown

We may or might have been being grown
You may or might have been being grown
They may or might have been being grown

Imperative
(You) be grown up (rarely used construction).

---

[1] Often contracted: I'd, you'd, we'd, he'd, she'd, they'd.
[2] Subjunctive mood, p.1

LINKING OR COPULATIVE VERBS

The linking or copulative verbs require subject complements (adjectives or nouns) to complete their meaning. The apples become . . . what? The adjective, *ripe* tells what became of the apples. (Note that you can always tell a linking verb by placing its complement in front of its subject. For example, The *ripe* apples.) Some linking verbs are referred to as *half-linking*[1] when they function actively as well. For example, dancers turn **quickly** *(adverb modifying the action of turn)* or dancers turn **pale** *(adjective,* complement describing the looks and telling what the subject became.)

When undergoing progressive form conjugations, some of these verbs may become semantically constrained, and the conjugations are limited to the logic of the entire sentence. Also there are some conjugations that are constrained and rarely used because of the awkward sounding alliteration, as in, *be being* or *been being*.

APPEAR[1]
BE
BECOME[2]
FEEL
GET[1] (become)
GROW[1]
KEEP[1]
LOOK[1]
PROVE
REMAIN
SEEM
SMELL
SOUND
STAND
TASTE
TURN[1] (become)

[1] A half-linking verb may take an adverb, for example, "They *gingerly* feel the stove top," or "That bloodhound smells *carefully*," *or* The soldiers *quickly* stand to attention."
[2] Usage requires *well* (functioning as an adjective) in matters of health or appearance. For example, "The sick child child becomes *well* by the sea," or "The dress becomes her *well*."

ABBREVIATIONS

The following abbreviations are in this text:

Amer.   American

Brit.   British

dial.   dialectical

lit.   literary

obs.   obsolete

p.p.   past participle

reg.   regular

WORKBOOK EXERCISES

UNIT I
SUBJECT AND VERB AGREEMENT

The underlined verb in each of the following sentences does not always agree with the subject. Write the correct form of the verb on the blank line. If the underlined verb agrees with the subject, do not write anything.

1. Every one of our hedges <u>need</u> _____ trimming.
2. Do you know where my box of pens <u>are</u> _____ .
3. Smoke from cars <u>pollutes</u> _____ the air.
4. A play or a concert <u>cost</u> _____ too much.
5. The radio <u>costs</u> _____ extra.
6. The windows <u>is</u> _____ broken.
7. Corn and wheat <u>grows</u> _____ well in this soil.
8. Either one of these buses <u>take</u> _____ you downtown.
9. An ace <u>count</u> _____ as eleven.
10. Where <u>is</u> _____ the needle and thread?
11. The officers <u>has</u> _____ a special job to do.
12. My father or my mother sometimes <u>helps</u> _____ me with my math.
13. This pencil <u>sell</u> _____ for one dollar.
14. <u>Are</u> _____ you ready to give your report?
15. The facts in this story <u>makes</u> _____ you think.

UNIT II

Change the verbs in parenthesis to the **present tense**. For example: She (ran) <u>runs</u>.

1. She (ran) _____ and then (trod) _____ carefully.
2. Although she (liked) _____ him, she (could not marry) _____ him.
3. Hopping down the road, the boy (cried) _____ , "Help".
4. In the course of my life, many things (broke) _____ .
5. Furthermore, I (wanted) _____ gold, not silver.
6. He (came) _____ ; he (saw) _____ ; he (conquered) _____ .
7. Even though she was a top executive, she (mowed) _____ her lawn, and she (sewed) _____ her own clothing.
8. The hot, not boiling, water (burnt/burned) _____ her hand.
9. The children (learnt/learned) _____ the most when you (told) _____ them the least.
10. When I (thought) _____ of the cosmos, I (felt) _____ whole.
11. In a student's life a lot (could) _____ happen in a day.
12. The cat (was) _____ not mine, but its collar and bell (were) _____ .
13. We (went) _____ home; (played) _____ poker; (drank) _____ vodka;

(ate) _____ lobster; and (listened) _____ to Beethoven.

14. Cream, butter, eggs, cheese and pork; these (were) _____ the foods I (avoided) _____.

15. My doctor (said) _____ that I (should) _____ not eat cakes, candy, sugar or fat.

16. Fraida (sped) _____ too fast and (hurt) _____ her wrist.

17. She (froze) _____ in horror when she (realized) _____ she (would) _____ spend the rest of her life that way.

18. Amat and Cassandra (left)_____ late, (drove) _____ fast and (caught) _____ their plane every time.

19. They (flew) _____ home in time for Christmas.

20. The bubble (burst) _____.

UNIT III

DIALOGUE A.

The following dialogues provide oral or written exercises.

Using the blank spaces in parenthesis, change the previously underlined verb to the **past tense.**

Scene: Children in the park.

KIMSA Why didn't you <u>bring</u> your bat?

MAT   I (   ) it yesterday.

KIMSA Well, so what? Did you <u>buy</u> balls?

MAT   Of course, I (   ) those. Here, <u>catch</u>. (throws the ball).

KIMSA (catches it) I (   ) it. Now let's stop <u>fighting</u> about everything.

MAT   You (   ) me—I just want to play hide-and-go-<u>seek</u>.

KIMSA I've (   ) you many times. Now it's my turn to <u>hide.</u>

MAT   No you (   ) last night. Now, I <u>think</u> it's my turn.

KIMSA And my Mother (   ) you're such a good sport. Wait 'til I <u>tell</u> her.

MAT   I thought you'd (   ) her already. Don't they <u>teach</u> you good sportsmanship in your school?

KIMSA Sure they (   ) us that! <u>I'm</u> a good sport when I don't care!

MAT   You (n't) yesterday and you cared too!

KIMSA Okay, you can hide! Now am I a good sport?

MAT   (Laughs and runs off.) Yes you are now!

DIALOGUE B

Using the blank spaces in parenthesis, change the previous verb to the **past tense.**

Scene: Two teenagers in a a park. Example:

ELDA: Feed it.

JOSE I fed it.

ELDA: Eat it.
JOSE I (   ) it.
ELDA: Drink that milk.
JOSE I (   ) it.
ELDA: Begin again.
JOSE I already (   ) it.
ELDA: Write to him.
JOSE I already (   ).
ELDA: Wring it.
JOSE I (   ) it.
ELDA: Ring it.
JOSE I (   ) it.
ELDA: Cast her.
JOSE I (   ) her yesterday.
ELDA: Shrink it.
JOSE I (   ) it.
ELDA: Sleep here.
JOSE I (   ) there last night.
ELDA: Throw it over here.
JOSE I (   ) it over there.
ELDA: Come here.
JOSE I (   ) there.
ELDA: Oh forget it.
JOSE I (   ) it already.
ELDA: Drive me home.
JOSE I (   ) you home.
ELDA: Bring your mother.
JOSE I (   ) my mother.
ELDA: Take your father.
JOSE I (   ) him.
ELDA: Try your sister.
JOSE I (   ) her already.
ELDA: Fly her home.
JOSE I (   ) her home.
ELDA: Flee from them.

JOSE I (   ) from them.

ELDA: Lead your horse.

JOSE I (   ) it.

ELDA: Lean there.

JOSE I (   ) there.

ELDA: Lend me it.

JOSE I (   ) it.

ELDA: Send me some.

JOSE I (   ) you some.

ELDA: Make them well.

JOSE I already (   ) them.

ELDA: Fling it.

JOSE I (   ) it.

ELDA: String that harp.

JOSE I (   ) it.

ELDA: Then string my beads.

JOSE I (   ) them.

ELDA: Run back.

JOSE I (   ) back.

ELDA: Catch that bus.

JOSE I (   ) it.

ELDA: Teach me that.

JOSE I (   ) you that.

ELDA: You must seek them out.

JOSE I (   ) them out.

ELDA: Sink it.

JOSE I (   ) it.

ELDA: Hold her baby.

JOSE I (   ) her baby.

ELDA: Swim there.

JOSE I (   ) there.

ELDA: Think fast.

JOSE I (   ) fast.

ELDA: Shred these.

JOSE I (   ) them.

ELDA: Put it down.

JOSE I (   ) it down.

ELDA: Sweep the floor.

JOSE I (   ) it.

ELDA: Go to dinner.

JOSE We (   ) to dinner.

ELDA: Show me.

JOSE I (   ) you.

ELDA: Get it?

JOSE I (   ) it.

ELDA: Say it.

JOSE I (   ) it.

ELDA: Lay it.

JOSE I (   ) it.

ELDA: Lie down.

JOSE I (   ) down.

ELDA: Rid me of it.

JOSE I (   ) you of it.

ELDA: Ride there.

JOSE I (   ) there last summer.

For an additional exercise, change the verbs in Dialogue B from the present indicative to the **present perfect tense.**

DIALOGUE C

Using the blank spaces in parenthesis, change the previously underlined word to the **past tense.** Note the auxiliaries *have* ('ve) *had* (d) or forms of *be* which require past participles.

Scene: Two mothers from New York are discussing their sons.

MRS. LEVINE I send (   ) all my hard earned savings to him, and what happens?

MRS. O'HARA Well, what (   )?

MRS. LEVINE He spends it gambling.

MRS. O'HARA If he (   ) it gambling, it's no worse than Paddie.

MRS. LEVINE Who could be worse? Does he spend money or lend it?

MRS. O'HARA Worse much worse. I (   ) him $500 and he <u>rends</u>[1] the envelope in two. **He never even** read my note.

MRS. LEVINE He (   ) it? Well, did he finally tape it together?

MRS. O'HARA No, it was the garbage collector's day.

MRS. LEVINE Well, that's still better than gambling it. I wish he'd <u>spend</u> it on a girl.

MRS. O'HARA If he (   ) it on the same one! Mine goes through ten a day. All he does is <u>shend</u>[2] me.

MRS. LEVINE They've (   ) us both for too long. Thank the Lord we have daughters.!

DIALOGUE D

Using the blank spaces in the parenthesis, change the previously underlined word to the **past tense.** Watch out for the auxiliaries have ('ve) or any form of *be* or *get*.

Scene: Two students in the cafeteria.

MARIA Did you <u>begin</u> school early?

CARLOS I (   ) school as soon as I could.

MARIA What? When you were still <u>drinking</u> milk?

CARLOS Yes, I've (   ) more milk than most people.

MARIA Milk, school . . . the two <u>go</u> together like peanut butter and jelly. That's all I ever **ate when I** (   ) to school. Well, I'm finished with all that! Now I work for a <u>shrink</u> and ring bells for a hobby.

CARLOS I saw a psychologist last year. He (   ) me once and that was enough <u>shrinking</u> for me.

MARIA He obviously hadn't (   ) you enough! I <u>ring</u> bells—it's cheaper.

CARLOS I (   ) a bell in the playground once.

MARIA I mean <u>ringing</u> church bells.

CARLOS That's a weird thing for a girl to do. How many bells have you (   )?

MARIA I'm working on it. So far I can do six at one time. It keeps me sane and it <u>keeps</u> me strong.

CARLOS I've (   ) strong by <u>swimming</u>.

MARIA I never (   ) much. How many laps can you <u>swim</u>?

CARLOS I've (   ) 100 laps.

MARIA Did you even swim from a <u>sinking</u> boat?

CARLOS Never, but my dad (   ) many.

MARIA What for real? Did he <u>sink</u> battleships?

CARLOS He (   ) one and before that he'd (   ) cruisers and submarines.

MARIA I bet the worst things about living on a ship are having rats and skunks that <u>stink</u> and no <u>drink</u>.

---

[1]rend: (literary) to tear
[2]shend: (dialectical) to shame

CARLOS When the skunk (   ), the sailors got (   ). Then their boats will <u>sink</u> and their uniforms will <u>shrink</u>.

MARIA Huh? You're crazy. If they'd got drunk and their boat had (   ), how would you know if their uniforms had (   )? Don't <u>spring</u> any more rhymes on me.

CARLOS I (   ) one; I've (   ) many. How about me <u>singing</u>?

MARIA I've rung bells and you've sprung rhymes but we've never (   ) songs together.

CARLOS (laughs) Okay.

UNIT IV

Changing Forms in Shoes, a Short Story by Valerie Hannah Weisberg

Change the verb in parenthesis to the **past tense**.

Carlos (wants) _____ a sombrero.

Juan (wants) _____ shoes. There are many, many miles between them.

Carlos (says) _____ "I don't want shoes. I have too many."

Juan (works) _____ hard in his village and (collects) _____ shells from the beach for his sister, Maria, to make necklaces. He also (picks) _____ up pieces of leather from the shoemaker's shop. One day, Juan (may) _____ collect enough to make a pair of shoes.

Carlos (goes) _____ to school. He (has) _____ many English speaking friends. He (plays) _____ with clay and blocks and (rides) _____ bicycles. He (likes) _____ school.

During the summer, Juan (is) _____ happy because many foreign people (come) _____ and (visit) _____ his village. He then (helps)_____ his father and (sells) _____ ice cream. He (sees) _____ all the children's shoes, and (works) _____ especially hard for his father. At the end of the day, when the sun (sinks) _____ under the sea, Juan's father (gives) _____ him a peso.

Carlos (has) _____ so many shoes that he (doesn't) _____ care and (hides) _____ them. His mother and father (are) _____ very angry, Carlos (explains) _____ to his mother that he (doesn't) _____ need shoes. When the sun (rises) _____ he (wants) _____ a sombrero. His mother (says) _____ , that he (will) _____ have no more treats and (sends) _____ him to bed. The next day Carlos (goes) _____ to school without shoes. The children (laugh) _____ at his bare feet. Carlos (becomes) _____ sad; he (doesn't) _____ like school anymore. That evening, Carlos (searches) _____ high and low. He (finds) _____ one shoe in his cupboard. He (discovers) _____ another in his toy chest and all the rest (are hidden) _____ in the trees and on the ivy slope.

Juan (works) _____ hard, but the shoemaker (tells) _____ him that it (will take) _____ a long time to save up enough pesos for a pair of shoes. Still, Juan (knows) _____ that one day he (will have saved) _____ enough.

Carlos (does not) _____ go to school during the summer vacation. Instead he (is going) _____ with his mama and papa to visit his grandma and grandpa in Guatemala. Carlos (likes) _____ his grandparents and (can't wait) _____ for the train ride. That night he (lies) _____ awake watching his parents pack. He (awakes) _____ early the next morning and (carries) _____ his suitcase onto the train. It (is) _____ a long journey.

While Carlos (is travelling) _____ all those miles, Juan (is working) _____ even harder. His sister Maria (gives) _____ him extra pesos as he (sells) _____ lots of her necklaces to the tourists, and the shoemaker (has given) _____ him extra pesos because he (sweeps) _____ the floor and (brings) _____ the tourists to his shop.

At last, Carlos (arrive) _____ in Guatemala. His grandparents (wait) _____ at the station to greet them. Carlos (gets) _____ lots of hugs and kisses. That night he (falls) _____ asleep at the dinner table.

Carlos's grandfather is a fisherman. The next morning Carlos (goes) _____ with his grandfather to set up the fishing tackle. His grandfather (leaves) _____ for three days. Carlos (feels) _____ sad. His grandpa (teaches) _____ Carlos about the tackle and (promises) _____ to teach him more when he (returns). _____

As he (walks) _____ along the beach he (starts) _____ picking up shells. He (meets) _____ Juan who (is also picking) _____ up shells.

They (make) _____ friends and Carlos (helps) _____ Juan collect more shells. Maria (is) _____ very happy with them and Juan's dad (gives) _____ Carlos an ice cream.

Carlos (looks) _____ at Juan's sombrero.

Juan (looks) _____ at Carlos's shoes.

Maria (laughs) _____ .

When the sun (sinks) _____ down under the sea, the two friends (separate) _____ ; Carlos (wears) _____ a sombrero. On Juan's feet (are) _____ blue shoes.

UNIT V

Changing Forms in a Poem by Valerie Hannah Weisberg

Change the verbs in parenthesis to **future perfect tense.**

China Doll

A China Doll (breaks) _____
You (curl) _____ its hair
You (wash) _____ its feet,
You (clothe) _____ it prettily and neat.
You (let) _____ the doll remain intact
Ensconced on a silver plate
But (you'll never know) _____
When she (will break) _____ .
So you (care) _____ and (care) _____
Then you (take) _____ that doll,
For what (she's) _____ worth,
And (lift) _____ her gently,

159

Or she'll (curse)_____.
Then when you (imprison) _____ her so neat,
That she cannot even meet
With people of her own kind,
To speak doll's talk in a doll land.
When you (make) _____ her live,
Or so it (seems) _____,
In a tower of strawberries and cream,

Then you (know) _____
That she (will go) _____
Or (break) _____ and (curse) _____ . . .
Oh how she (will curse) _____!

UNIT VI

Changing Forms in a Passage from *Dombey and Sons* by Charles Dickens

Change verb stem in parentheses to, in part, the **present perfect tense.** Use what you think most appropriate for the style and meaning of the passage. Some should be in the Passive Voice.

(Railway Construction in a London Suburb)

The first shock of a great earthquake (have) _____ just at that period, (rend) _____ the whole neighborhood to its center. Traces of its course (be) _____ visible on every side. Houses (knock) _____ down; streets (broke) _____ through and (stop) _____; deep pits and trenches (dig) _____ in the ground; enormous heaps of earth and clay (throw)) _____ up; buildings that (undermine) _____ and (shake) _____ (prop) _____ by great beams of wood. Here a chaos of carts, overthrown and jumbled together, (lie) _____ topsy turvy at the bottom of a steep unnatural hill; there, confused treasures of iron (soak) _____ and (rust) _____ in something that (become) _____ accidentally a pond. Everywhere there (be) _____ bridges that (lead) _____ nowhere; thoroughfares that (be) _____ wholly impassable; and Babel towers of chimneys, wanting half their height; temporary wooden houses and enclosures, in the most unlikely situations; carcasses of ragged tenements, and fragments of unfinished walls and arches, and piles of scaffolding, and wildernesses of bricks and giant forms of cranes, and tripods (straddle) _____ above nothing.

In short, the yet unfinished and unopened Railroad (be) _____ in progress; and from the very core of all this dire disorder, (trail) _____ smoothly away, upon its mighty course of civilization and improvement.

Charles Dickens wrote this in England in 1846, a high point in the railway boom. This passage from Chapter VI pictures a housing complex called "Stagg's Gardens" in Camden Town, then considered a suburb of London.

UNIT VII

In the following passage adapted from *Ecclesiastes*, change the verb form to the **conditional perfect tense.**

1. I (think) _____ and (see) _____ that the race (is) _____ not to the swift, nor the battle to the strong, neither yet bread to the wise, nor yet favor to men of skill, but that time and chance (happen) _____ to us all.

Now change to the **future perfect tense.**

2. I (consider) _____ and (understand) _____ that the race (is) _____ not to the swift, nor the battle to the strong, neither yet bread to the wise, nor yet favor to men of skill, but that time and chance (occur) _____ to us all.

Now change the form to the **conditional perfect progressive tense.**

3. I dream) _____ and (perceive) _____ that the race (is) _____ not to the swift, nor the battle to the strong, neither yet bread to the wise, nor yet favor to men of skill, but that time and chance (happen) _____ to us all.

Now change the verb form to the **past tense.**

4. I (realize) _____ and (see) _____ that the race (is) _____ not to the swift, nor the battle to the strong, neither yet bread to the wise, nor yet favor to men of skill, but that time and chance (happen) _____ to us all.

Now change the verb form to the **subjunctive past perfect tense.**

5. I (know) _____ and (believe) _____ and (see) _____ that the race (is) _____ not to the swift, nor the battle to the strong, neither yet bread to the wise, nor yet favor to men of skill, but that time and chance (occur) _____ to us all.

Now change to the **future perfect tense.**

6. I (awake) _____ and (rise) _____ and (see) _____ that the race (is) _____ not to the swift, nor the battle to the strong, neither yet bread to the wise, nor yet favor to men of skill, but that time and chance (happen) _____ to us all.

Now change the form to the **future progressive tense.**

7. I (ride) _____ and (see) _____ that the race (is) _____ not to the swift, nor the battle to the strong, neither yet bread to the wise, nor yet favor to men of skill, but that time and chance (occur) _____ to us all.

UNIT I Subject and Verb Agreement

1. needs 2. is 3. pollutes 4. costs 5. costs 6. are 7. grow 8. takes 9. counts 10. are 11. have 12. helps 13. sells 14. Are 15. make

Unit II

1. runs, treads 2. likes, cannot marry 3. cries 4. break 5. want 6. comes, sees, conquers 7. mows, sews 8. burns 9. learn, tell 10. think, feel 11. can 12. is, are 13. go, play, drink, eat, listen 14. are, avoid 15. says, shall 16. speeds, hurts 17. freezes, realizes, will 18. leave, drive, catch 19. fly 20. bursts

UNIT III
Dialogue A

brought, bought, caught, fought, sought, hid, thought, told, taught, were.

Dialogue B

ate, drank, began, wrote, wrung, rang, cast, shrank, slept, threw, came, forgot, drove, brought, took, tried, flew, fled, led, leant/leaned, lent, sent, made, flung, stringed, strung, ran, caught, taught, sought, sank, held, swam, thought, shred/shredded, put, swept, went, showed, got, said, laid, lay, rid, rode

Dialogue C

sent, happened, spent, lent, rent, spent, shent

Dialogue D

began, drunk, went, shrank, shrunk, rang, rung, kept, swam, swum, sank, sank, sunk, stunk, drunk, sunk, shrunk, sprang, sprung, sung

UNIT IV

wanted, wanted, said, worked, collected, picked, might, went, had, played, rode, liked, was, came, visited, helped, sold, saw, worked, sank, gave, had, didn't, hid, were, explained, didn't, rose, wanted, said, would, sent, went, laughed, became, didn't, searched, found, discovered, were hidden, worked, told, would take, knew, would have saved, did not or didn't, was going, liked, couldn't wait, lay, awoke, carried, was, was travelling, was working, gave, sold, had given, swept, brought, arrived, waited, got, fell, went, left, felt, taught, promised, returned, walked, started, met, was also picking, made, helped, was, gave, looked, looked, laughed, sank, separated, wore, were

UNIT V

will have broken, will have curled, will have washed, will have clad/clothed, will have let, you will never have known, will have broken, will have cared, cared or will have cared, will have taken, will have been, will have lifted, have cursed, will have imprisoned, will have made, will have seemed, will have known, will have gone, will have broken, will have cursed, will have cursed

UNIT VI

has . . . rent, are, are knocked, broken or are broken, stopped, are dug, are thrown, undermine or have undermined, and shake or have shaken or are or have been shaken, are propped, lie or have lain, have soaked or soak, have rusted or rust, has become or became, are, have led or lead, are or have been, are straddling or straddle, is, is trailing or trails

UNIT VII

1. could, should or would have thought and could, should or would have seen or seen, could, should or would have been, could, should or would have happened.
2. will have considered and will have understood or understood, will have been, will have occurred.
3. could, should, or would have been dreaming and could, should, or would have been perceiving or perceiving, could, should, or would not have been, could, should, or would have been happening
4. realized, saw was, happened.
5. might have known and might have believed or believed, might have seen or seen, might not have been , might have occurred
6. will have awoken or awaked or awoke and will have risen or risen, will have seen or seen, will not have been, will have happened
7. will be riding and will be seeing or seeing, will be (being[3]), will be occurring

ANSWER KEY

---

[3]Semantically constrained, see be in text.

VERB SCRAMBLERS

Forms of irregular and regular verbs can be found in the scrambler. Only count the verb and its forms. For example, BEGIN has two other verbs, BE and BEG the other two words, *gin* and *in* should not be counted. Verbs are printed horizontally, vertically, and diagonally. The initial letter can be used for more than one word:

```
        L
  B E G I N
  T A O
        T
```

Here, BEGIN, BE, BAT, and BEG, (verbs sharing B) LET, GOT and GO make a possible verb score of 7.

How many verbs can you find in the following scramblers?

B	E	R	E	F	T	D	K	N	I	T	A	K	E	A
L	E	F	T	O	R	N	E	S	T	A	I	N	G	S
A	G	S	E	E	K	O	W	A	S	K	E	E	P	K
D	R	E	W	R	I	T	E	S	T	E	A	W	I	T
D	U	G	T	T	E	S	T	R	E	W	A	S	E	E
W	E	A	V	E	S	S	W	A	T	E	S	T	E	R
E	V	D	L	W	R	I	T	T	E	N	S	K	I	P
T	R	Y	L	E	N	P	E	A	L	N	S	V	A	I
S	E	E	P	E	E	L	I	V	E	G	T	I	E	D
K	I	S	S	P	T	R	E	A	D	E	C	S	T	V
N	A	G	I	N	B	R	E	D	E	H	L	T	I	E
I	O	S	S	E	E	A	D	E	P	A	R	T	E	O
T	E	E	N	T	R	E	A	T	S	D	O	U	B	T
S	E	N	T	A	K	E	E	R	O	D	E	B	I	T
D	A	M	A	G	E	D	I	T	E	O	W	E	N	D

B	E	R	E	A	V	E	D	K	N	I	T	A	K	E
L	E	F	T	O	R	N	E	S	T	A	I	N	G	S
A	G	R	E	E	S	O	W	A	S	K	E	A	T	K
D	R	A	W	R	I	T	E	S	T	O	R	E	S	T
D	I	G	A	V	E	S	T	L	O	W	A	A	S	K
W	E	S	V	E	S	S	W	A	Y	C	S	G	E	T
E	V	D	O	L	I	T	T	V	E	S	K	N	O	W
P	E	T	A	W	T	A	R	E	C	U	P	T	O	T
T	R	Y	L	E	N	P	E	A	L	N	S	V	A	I
M	E	E	T	E	L	L	O	V	E	G	E	T	E	N
K	I	S	S	P	T	R	E	A	D	E	C	S	T	V
N	A	G	I	N	B	R	E	D	E	H	L	T	I	E
T	O	S	S	E	E	A	D	E	P	A	R	T	E	S
B	E	E	N	T	R	E	A	D	D	O	U	B	T	
W	E	N	T	T	A	K	E	E	R	O	D	E	T	E

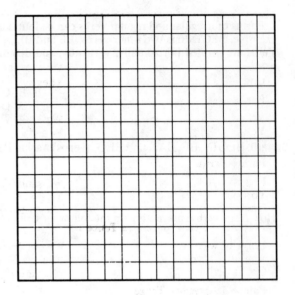

A	D	V	I	S	E	T	T	L	E	S	W	O	R	E
D	E	E	D	O	E	S	A	W	A	K	E	A	I	T
D	I	P	C	L	E	A	V	E	T	O	R	E	S	P
D	A	N	C	E	A	S	E	R	E	V	E	A	L	I
W	E	E	P	S	A	V	E	Y	W	E	R	E	A	P
E	V	D	E	L	E	T	S	A	T	R	A	S	T	E
N	E	T	A	S	T	E	P	E	R	U	S	T	O	P
D	R	Y	L	I	A	V	S	T	A	N	A	W	A	R
P	A	I	D	T	O	L	D	R	O	V	E	P	I	T
E	K	E	A	S	I	T	R	E	A	T	N	A	I	L
T	R	I	P	E	E	L	Y	I	D	O	N	E	A	M
T	O	O	K	N	E	L	T	D	E	A	L	T	A	R
B	E	O	P	E	N	T	G	R	A	T	E	I	O	B
W	A	N	T	K	E	D	R	I	D	I	T	E	A	T
B	E	H	E	A	V	E	D	D	D	E	E	D	A	M

Most of the following verb stems or their forms can be found in the scramblers: (High achievers with scores above 40, may find other verbs not listed.)

ADD ADVISE AID AGE AWAKE BEAR BITE BIT CARE CLEAVE DANCE DELIVER DIP DEAL DEED DIE DIG DO DOTE DOUBT DRAW DRY EAT ERASE GAVE GO GROW KEEP KISS LEAVE LIVE LOSE LOOSE MEET MOW NAG NET OPEN PAT PEAL PEEL PEEP RENT REST REV REVEAL RUST READ REAP REPEAL ROT SAVE SIT SEE SEEK SELL SETTLE SING SNEAK SKID SPIT STARE STORE STROW SWAY SWEAR TAKE TAN TAP TELL TIE TIRE TOP TRAP TREAD TREAT TOY TRAIL TREAT TREK TWIST WANT WAR WAVE WEAR WEAVE WEEP YELL YELP

Past Participles:

VERB FORM

Indicative Present Tense

VERB STEM[1]

I	We
You	You
One[2]	They

Past Tense

I	We
You	You
One	They

Future Tense

I[3] shall	We shall
You will	You will
One will	They will

Present or Past Progressive Tense

I[4] am or was	We are or were
You are or were	You are or were
One is or was	They are or were

Future Progressive Tense

I shall be	We shall be
You will be	You will be
One will be	They will be

Present or Past Perfect Tense

I[5] have or had	We have or had
You have or had	You have or had
One has or had	They have or had

Future Perfect Tense

I[3] shall have	We shall have
You will have	You will have
One will have	They will have

Future Perfect Progressive Tense

I shall have been	We shall have been
You will have been	You will have been
One will have been	They will have been

---

[1] Same conjugations for
[2] Also she, he, it.
[3] Often contracted: I'll, you'll, he'll, she'll, we'll, or they'll (shall not: shan't, will not: won't).
[4] Often contracted: I'm, you're, we're, or they're.
[5] Often contracted: I've or I'd, you've or you'd, we've or we'd, or they've or they'd.

Present or Past Perfect Progressive Tense

I have or had been
You have been
One has or had been

We have or had been
You have or had been
They have or had been

Conditional (would, should or could)

I[1] would
You would
One would

We would
You would
They would

Conditional Progressive Tense

I would be
You would be
One would be

We would be
You would be
They would be

Conditional Perfect Tense

I would have
You would have
One would have

We would have
You would have
They would have

Conditional Perfect Progressive Tense

I would have been
You would have been
One would have been

We would have been
You would have been
They would have been

Subjunctive Present or Past Tense

I may or might
You may or might
One may or might

We may or might
You may or might
They may or might

Subjunctive Present or Past Perfect Tense

I may[2] or might have
You may or might have
One may or might have

We may or might have
You may or might have
They may or might have

Subjunctive Present or Past Perfect Progressive Tense

I may or might have been
You may or might have been
One may or might have been

We may or might have been
You may or might have been
They may or might have been

Imperative:

(You)   (it).

---

[1] Often contracted: I'd, you'd, we'd, he'd, she'd, they'd.
[2] Subjunctive mood, p.1

Indicate the right tenses for each of the following illustrations:

1. _____

2. _____

3. _____

4. _____

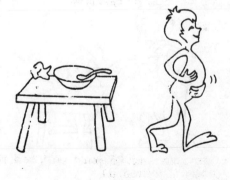

5. _____

6. _____

7. _____

8. _____

9. _____

10. _____